a brief history of the future

ALSO BY JACQUES ATTALI

The Labyrinth in Culture and Society: Pathways to Wisdom

A Man of Influence: The Extraordinary Career of S. G. Warburg

Millennium: Winners and Losers in the Coming World Order

Noise: The Political Economy of Music

a brief history of the future

a brief history of the future

a brave and controversial look
at the twenty-first century

jacques attali

translated from the french
by jeremy leggatt

arcade publishing
new york

FIRST ENGLISH-LANGUAGE EDITION

First published in French as *Une brève histoire de l'avenir* by Librairie Arthème Fayard

Library of Congress Cataloging-in-Publication Data

Attali, Jacques.
[Brève histoire de l'avenir. English]
A brief history of the future : a brave and controversial look at the twenty-first century / Jacques Attali ; translated from the French by Jeremy Leggatt. —1st English-language ed.
p. cm.
ISBN 978-1-55970-879-1 (alk. paper)
1. World politics—21st century—Forecasting. 2. Economic forecasting. 3. Twenty-first century—Forecasts. I. Title.
D863.A8813 2009
303.49—dc22 2008031203

Published in the United States by Arcade Publishing, Inc., New York
Distributed by Hachette Book Group

Visit our Web site at www.arcadepub.com
Visit the author's Web site at www.attali.com

10 9 8 7 6 5 4 3 2 1

Designed by API

EB

PRINTED IN THE UNITED STATES OF AMERICA

Alas! It is delusion all;
The future cheats us from afar,
Nor can we be what we recall,
Nor dare we think on what we are.

—Lord Byron, “Stanzas for Music”

Contents

Foreword

As I write this, the shape of the world in 2050 and its likely configuration in 2100 are being determined. Depending on how we act today, our children and grandchildren will either inherit an enhanced, habitable world or else will toil, loathing us, in a sort of hell. To ensure that we hand down to them a livable planet, we must start thinking now about what the future holds. We must strive to understand the origins of that future, and what needs to be done to help shape it.

One may doubt, or scoff at, the very notion of anyone daring to predict the future even twenty-five, fifty, or especially a hundred years from now. So many imponderables, so many unanticipated events or people will intervene between now and then to change the course of history.

A few examples should make this clear. If Napoleon Bonaparte had not ascended over his contemporaries in 1799, the French Revolution might have given birth to a parliamentary republic and stolen a whole century from history. If an assassin in Sarajevo had missed his target in 1914, the First World War would probably not have broken out — or at least not in the same way. If Hitler had not invaded Russia in 1941, he might have died in power and in his bed, like Spain's General Franco. If Japan, in the same year, had attacked Russia instead of the United States, America might not have entered the war and liberated Europe, just as in real life it never went on to liberate either Spain or Poland—and France, Italy, and the rest of Europe might have remained under the Nazi heel at least until the end of the 1970s. And finally, if the general secretary of the Soviet Communist Party had not died prematurely in 1984, and if his successor's successor had been—as was planned—Grigory Romanov rather than Mikhail Gorbachev, the Soviet Union might well still be in existence. Still, as I believe I shall demonstrate, if we first look back before looking forward, we shall see that history obeys laws that allow us to make predictions and channel its course.

Here is where the history of the future, by definition unpredictable, begins. So many coincidences could transform a local incident into a planetary episode, so many people could affect geopolitics, culture, ideology, and the economy that one may even doubt the very questions we might ask ourselves about the future, even that closest to us. Here are a few specific questions we need to ponder and address in the near term:

- Will peace in the Middle East one day be possible?
- Will global birth rates in some countries recover as mysteriously as they declined?
- Will oil supplies run out in twenty or fifty years?

- Will we find substitute energy sources?
- Will poverty and inequalities in wealthy countries become the wellspring for new violence?
- Will Arab countries one day experience a democratic movement like that of Eastern Europe?
- Will the Straits of Hormuz and Malacca, through which the bulk of the world's oil flows, be blocked by ships sunk by pirates?
- Will North Korea end up using nuclear weapons?
- Will the West use force to prevent Iran from acquiring them?
- Will a terrorist attack in the West topple a government?
- Will it lead to the installation of authoritarian police regimes?
- Will new technologies make new forms of dictatorship possible?
- Will religions become tolerant?
- Will we discover new ways of doing away with cancer, AIDS, obesity?
- Will a dominant new religion or ideology emerge?
- Will the exploited workers in Chinese or

Bangladeshi mines rise up in revolt?

- Will the American credit crisis plummet the world into another great depression?
- Will genetically modified food or nanotechnologies prove a threat or an opportunity?
- Will the climate one day be so degraded that life on earth becomes impossible?
- Will a religious war once again pit Christianity against Islam?
- Will new forms of sexual relations undermine morality?

The answers to each of these questions — and many more — will direct the coming decades on a very particular course, for better or worse. This is in fact the peculiarity of the times ahead: a glaringly obvious instability and such rooted interdependence that any revolt, any new idea, any technological progress, any terrorist act, any coup d'état, or any scientific discovery could change the world's course. Any one of these events might impede the circulation of ideas, goods, capital, and people — and therefore of growth, jobs, and freedom.

Yet most of these events will have only a fleeting impact on the world's development. For beyond the problems that today seem major and will one day be resolved (we shall see later on in detail what obstacles have to be overcome), other powerful movements, seemingly unchanging, will continue their work.

Viewed from an extremely long-range standpoint,

history flows in a single, stubborn, and very particular direction, which no upheaval, however long-lasting, can permanently deflect: *from century to century, humankind has asserted the primacy of individual freedom over all other values.* It has done so through progressive rejection of all forms of servitude, through technical advances aimed at minimizing human effort, and through liberalization of lifestyles, political systems, art, and ideologies. To put it another way: human history relates the individual's assumption of his rights as an entity legally empowered to plan and master his fate free of all constraints—except respect for the right of his fellow man to the same freedoms.

I predict that in the course of the twenty-first century, market forces will take the planet in hand. The ultimate expression of unchecked individualism, this triumphant march of money explains the essence of history's most recent convulsions. It is up to us to accelerate, resist, or master it.

Carried through to term, this evolutionary process means that money will finally rid itself of everything that threatens it—including nation-states (and not excepting the United States of America), which it will progressively dismantle. Once the market becomes the world's only universally recognized law, it will evolve into what I shall call *super-empire*, an entity whose structures remain elusive but whose reach is global.

If—even before it struggles free of its past alienations—humankind balks at such a future and cuts short the process of globalization through violence, it could well fall back into barbarous, devastating wars, pitting nations, religious groups, terrorist entities, and free-market pirates against one another. I shall call this era of struggle *hyperconflict*.

Finally, if globalization can be contained rather than rejected, if the market can be held in check without being abolished, if democracy can spread planetwide while remaining accessible to all, if imperial domination of the world can be brought to an end, then a universe of infinite possibilities will be within reach, an era of freedom, responsibility, dignity, transcendence, respect for others, and altruism. I shall call this era *hyperdemocracy*. It will culminate in the creation of a democratic world government and an assortment of local and regional institutions of governance. Through future technologies, it will empower everyone to advance toward disinterestedness and abundance, sharing equitably in the benefits of the commercial imagination, protecting the freedom of its own excesses as well as those of its enemies, bequeathing a better-protected environment to coming generations, and—with all the world's accumulated forms of wisdom—generating new ways of living and creating together.

These market forces, this mercantile freedom, has already contributed to the birth of political freedom. Its first beneficiaries were a privileged minority. Then (on paper at least) the privilege was extended to the many and across ever-expanding territories, displacing religious or military power almost everywhere. In short, dictatorships give birth to the market, which in turn engenders democracy. Thus, in the twelfth century of our era, the first *market democracies* were born.

By slow but steady degrees, their geographical

space expanded. The centers of power in the regions controlling these market democracies gradually shifted westward. The twelfth century saw the center of market democracy move from the Middle East to the Mediterranean, then to the North Sea, the Atlantic Ocean, and finally to where it holds sway today: the Pacific region of North America. Later I shall pinpoint the twelve cores, or world mercantile leaders, as history has moved steadily westward.

If this millennia-long history continues to unfold over the next half century, markets and democracy will expand wherever they are still absent. Growth will accelerate, standards of living will improve. Dictatorship will vanish from those countries where it still holds sway. All toward the good. But on the other hand, water and energy will become scarcer, and the climate will be further endangered. The gap between rich and poor will widen, leading to aggravated social tensions. Conflicts will flare, and vast population movements will begin.

After a very long struggle and in the midst of a serious ecological crisis, the still dominant empire—the United States—will finally be defeated around 2035 by this same globalization of the markets (particularly the financial ones), and by the power of corporations. Financially and politically exhausted, like all other empires before it, the United States will cease to run the world. But it will remain the planet's major power; no new empire or dominant nation will replace it. The world will temporarily become *polycentric*, with a dozen or so regional powers managing its affairs.

By 2060 at the earliest—unless the human race has disappeared beneath a deluge of bombs—neither the

American empire, nor hyperempire, nor hyperconflict will be conceivable. Driven by ecological, ethical, economic, cultural, or political necessity, new forces, altruistic and universalizing, will seize the reins all over the world. They will rebel against the tyranny of monitoring, of narcissism, and of norms. They will lead steadily toward a new balance (planetary this time) between the market and democracy—hyperdemocracy. Exploiting ever newer technologies, global or continental institutions will organize collective living, imposing limits on the production of commercial artifacts, on transforming life, and on the mercantile exploitation of natural resources. They will prefer freedom of action, responsibility, and access to knowledge. They will usher in the birth of a *universal intelligence*, making common property of the creative capacities of all human beings in order to transcend them. A new, synchronized economy, providing free services, will develop in competition with the market before eliminating it, exactly as the market put an end to feudalism a few centuries ago.

Like every summary, the foregoing might seem arbitrary, even pat, a mere self-caricature. Yet the whole object of this book is to demonstrate that this represents the most probable face of the future. Readers familiar with my work will again encounter (in more fully elaborated form) theories articulated in my earlier essays and novels. In them I predicted (well before they became common coin) the world's geopolitical tilt toward the Pacific; the financial instability of capitalism, culminating in the increasingly dangerous financial bubbles that have or soon will become global; climate issues; the fragility of communism; terrorist threats; the arrival of nomadic forces, which I shall explain and elaborate on later; and the major role of art—particularly of music—in fostering global diversity. Attentive readers will note certain changes in my thinking—which after all (and most fortunately) did not descend from heaven in finished form.

And finally, since every prediction is first and foremost a meditation on the present, this essay is also a political work. I hope that you will be able to use it to your best advantage at a time when so many major choices are looming.

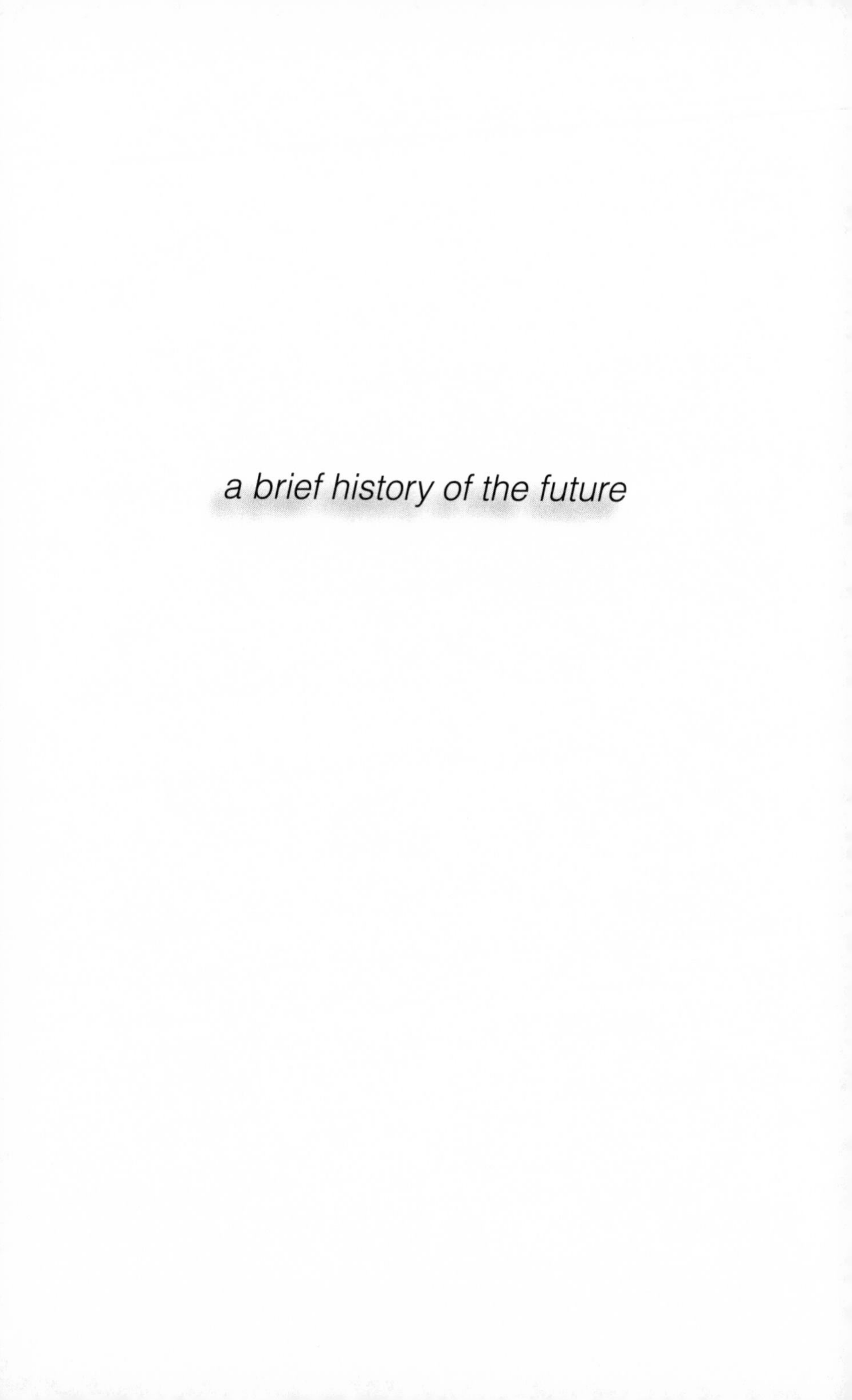

a brief history of the future

1

A Very Long History

To elaborate on what the future may hold, I must first paint — in broad strokes — the history of the past. We shall see that it is shot through with invariables, that history possesses a kind of structure which allows us to foresee the architecture of the decades ahead.

Since the dawn of time, every human group has formed around a source of wealth, a language, a territory, a philosophy, or a leader. Three powers have always coexisted: the religious, which sets the hours of prayer, marks the agricultural seasons, and moderates access to the afterlife; the military, which organizes the hunt, defense, and conquest; and the mercantile, which produces, finances, and markets the fruits of human labor. Each of these powers masters time by controlling the instruments for measuring it — astronomical observatories, hourglasses, and clocks.

In every human cosmogony, three gods overshadow all the others, elevating a dominant trinity to the apex of power: the Romans called them Jupiter, Mars, and Quirinus — the god of gods, the god of war, and the god of money. Below them was the domain of ordinary men. And below them, a different power existed within and alongside all the others, and may one day displace them all—the power of the feminine, which ensures the succession of the generations and presides over the transmission of knowledge.

Turn by turn, each of the three dominant powers (religious, military, and mercantile) controls wealth. Thus we may tell the history of humankind as the succession of three great political orders: the *ritual order*, in which authority is essentially religious; the *imperial order*, in which power is primarily military; and the *mercantile order*, in which the paramount group is the one that controls the economy. The first group's ideal is theological, the second's territorial, while the third's is individualistic.

In each of these orders, a society remains stable so long as the dominant group controls the distribution of wealth. Within the ritual order, this wealth pays for sacrifices; in the imperial order, it finances monument building; in the mercantile order, it goes into productive investments. And in all three orders, defense of executive power is a priority. Control of wealth by the dominant group is threatened by wars, natural disasters, external levies, and competition. To retain its hold on power, the dominant group seeks to implement a technical improvement to its own advantage, to exploit the weak, or to expand the space it dominates. If it fails, another dominant group takes its place.

Then, when even the legitimacy of its authority is challenged, a new order is established, with new powers, new knowledge, new ways of expending its surpluses, new geopolitical power relationships. Turn by turn, the master becomes the slave, the soldier replaces the priest, the merchant replaces the soldier.

Naturally, such evolutions do not proceed in neat stages: at every moment the three centers of power coexist, with premature advances and retreats.

Here now is the history of these orders and the manner of their birth and decline. From this account, extrapolating from facts seemingly trivial and insignificant, we will be able to identify the laws of history. It is essential that we understand these laws, for they will still be at work in the future and will enable us to predict its course.

Nomadism, Cannibalism, Sexuality

To establish these laws we must start from our very earliest knowledge of humankind. This will enable us to understand that the same power—that of man's progressive liberation from every constraint—is still on the march.

Some 3.8 billion years ago, life emerges in the ocean depths, and 350 million years ago on dry land. Around seven million years ago, according to the most recent discoveries, two early primates (Toumai in Chad and *Orrorin* in Kenya) climb down from the trees—doubtless after a drought—and stand upright on their two legs. Two million years later, another genus of primate, *Australopithecus*, also comes down from the trees to walk the landscapes of eastern and southern Africa. Three million years later, in the same region, certain of its descendants, *Homo habilis* and *Homo rudolfensis*, creatures selected by the demands of bipedal movement, adopt a more upright posture, and can therefore support a heavier brain. Gatherers, scavengers, and parasites, they learn to chip stones for use as tools, and begin their walk from territory to territory across the African continent.

The only survivors are the primates best adapted to wandering; the only progress comes through hunter-gatherer techniques compatible with movement.

A million and a half years ago, still in East Africa and shoulder to shoulder with primate species already in existence, *Homo ergaster* appears. He is even better adapted than the others to long journeys. Still somewhat stooped in stance, he is shaped by movement: he loses his fur and he can run. He even seems to have acquired the rudiments of speech.

A million years later a descendant of *Homo ergaster* evolves and gives birth to another species of primate: the very first to leave East Africa. In the space of a few dozen millennia, he explores the rest of Africa, Europe, Central Asia, India, Indonesia, and China.

A hundred thousand years later, two other primates are born (most likely still in Africa) — *Homo sapiens* and *Homo heidelbergensis*, still nomadic, and even better adapted for walking than their predecessors. They hold themselves more upright, they possess larger brains, and they boast greater sophistication in language. Their only tools are still chipped flint. Utterly at the mercy of the forces of nature, of rain, wind, and thunder, they see in those phenomena the manifestation of superior powers. They do not yet bury their dead, but their still precarious dwellings become stronger. All these primates — neighbors but not kin — coexist without interbreeding.

Unlike any other animal species, they begin to transmit knowledge from generation to generation. Lesson for the future: transmission is a condition of progress.

Around 700,000 years before our era, in China and Africa, *Homo sapiens* masters the lightning and learns how to make fire. He is now capable of cooking vegetables, thus providing better nourishment for his brain. He also realizes that he can summon certain natural forces to his service. This is a considerable leap. He devises the first footwear, sews man's first garments, and penetrates Europe, that cold, forest-shrouded continent.

The lineage of *Homo sapiens* splits into several branches. One of them evolves into *Homo neandertalis.* Around 300,000 years ago, he roams across Africa, Europe, and Asia. For the first time, he builds sophisticated huts wherever he goes, and he buries his dead. In Europe, still cut off by Alpine and Baltic glaciers, Neanderthals coexist with the other primates, neither mingling with nor replacing them.

It was doubtless at this time (300,000 years ago) that cannibalism began, not as an act of violence but as a ritual appropriation of the strength of the dead. Even today, we detect its vestiges in the human relationship with all levels of consumption. *Homo sapiens* also discovers that procreation is a consequence of the sex act, and that both partners have a role to play. The status of the sexes is now more clearly defined. Males live together, never changing tribes. Women, on the other hand—perhaps to avoid the incest that might weaken the group—leave the tribe at puberty, or at least distance themselves from it in order to have a space of their own, perhaps inside the tribal territory. Sexuality and reproduction start to be viewed separately, and a baleful historical chapter begins.

Around 160,000 years ago, still in Africa and on another evolutionary branch of *Homo sapiens*, the first modern man appears, the physical and intellectual fruit of the demands levied on nomads — *Homo sapiens sapiens.* His brain is much more sophisticated than that of the other primates. He is organized into vaster groups, in which women are responsible for raising children. For him everything is living. He buries his dead, and cannibalism is no doubt still very prevalent. Average life expectancy is less than twenty-five years. In the Middle East as in Europe, human groups wander. They accumulate nothing, save nothing, keep nothing in reserve. They own nothing that cannot be transported — fire, tools, weapons, clothing, knowledge, languages, rites, stories. Now begins trading in objects, women, and prisoners — the first markets. And no doubt the beginnings of slavery.

Around 85,000 years ago, the world climate becomes colder, and *Homo sapiens sapiens* builds less rudimentary shelters in which he lives for longer periods. He travels less and still coexists with several other species of primate. These diverse primates fight one another for shelter, women, or hunting areas. Their conflicts obey a few simple principles, their authenticity established for us in rediscovered vestiges — terrify, launch surprise attacks, cut the enemy's lines of communication, leave him no respite. Betraying allies is common, and so are engaging in simulated flight and attacking from behind. Cannibalism is still abroad, its aim still ingestion of the strength of the ancestors and ritualization of the human relationship with death. Eating life to evade death, an instinct that still prevails today.

About 45,000 years ago, the primate lives in caves in winter and spends his summers in huts. He makes increasingly specialized tools. Work is divided among members of the group — and with it comes unemployment for those who no longer directly produce their own food.

About the same time, the climate warms. Like the other animals, primates leave their shelters and begin to wander again. Now *Homo sapiens sapiens* penetrates Europe, Asia, and even Australia, which (in an extraordinary marine pilgrimage reaching far beyond the horizon) might already have been visited by other primates. He also reaches the Americas, perhaps by crossing the land bridge on the Bering Strait. In Europe, one branch of *Homo sapiens sapiens* (now known as Cro-Magnon man) encounters *Homo neandertalis*, who has been there for 250,000 years and is dominant everywhere. These diverse primates coexist for more than ten millennia, still wandering over vast territories they leave only in case of dire need.

Thirty thousand years ago, quite rapidly and without our knowing exactly why, every species of primate (including *Homo neandertalis*) vanishes — with the exception of *Homo sapiens sapiens.*

Henceforth he alone will be able to transmit his knowledge from generation to generation. Man's history can begin. Everything that he has learned until now, over two million years, will serve him to build what we are. And what we will become.

Ritualization, Sedentarization

At that moment, 30,000 years ago, certain humans begin to dream of an ideal afterworld, where every form of scarcity has disappeared and where they will be able to meet their ancestors. At the same time, the idea of a supreme and vital power emerges, of a God who at first stands alone. Cannibalism begins to lose ground to its own ritualization in religious sacrifice — devouring the body of a man sent to God in hopes of drawing closer to Him. Notions of ownership are clarified; languages diversify; work divisions become more complicated. One builds huts, another sews clothing or carves stones, while still others manufacture tools and weapons, hunt, tell stories, care for one another, pray. Men seize power over women, giving responsibility over their mothers and sisters to brothers and cousins. Vetoes evolve, making it possible to curtail violence. Members of a group still help one another, work together, raise their children together, eat meals together. But they can no longer hunt or gather, or communally consume certain animals and certain plants declared taboo, nor above all can they enjoy sexual relations among themselves — for since incest is forbidden, women can remain within the group. Lesson for the future: the sacred legitimizes taboos.

Life expectancy has risen above thirty years. Man begins finding time to share what he knows with future generations. This wish to transmit is also what increasingly sets him apart from all other animal species.

Man slowly learns to split the idea of God into several categories, dictated by His various manifestations in nature — fire, wind, earth, rain, and so on. Polytheism is thus a religious construct inherited from a primitive monotheism. And the sacred helps found policy. The ritual order begins. Now man envisages accompanying his dead into the afterlife in sophisticated tombs with ceremonies, offerings, sacrifices to the deceased. His aim is to win from the gods (whom he will shortly encounter) a promise of protection for the living. In each clan or tribe, a leader — simultaneously priest and healer — masters violence by assigning to each person a particular relationship with the sacred. Every chief is master of taboos, of the calendar, of hunting, and of force. Cosmogonies designate scapegoats, who also serve as intermediaries with the beyond. Song and flute music are the first means of communicating with these intermediaries. Labyrinths are the first metaphoric representations of these voyages.

Objects made by men are, in primitive societies, seen as living beings, children of their makers. Trading them, seeking to establish equivalencies among them, is like the exchange of slaves, hostages, or women. Virtually everywhere on earth, this trade in manufactured objects becomes a kind of hostage exchange — a source of violence if left uncurbed. It is often, in many cultures, ritualized by the duty of silence imposed on participants in the exchange: the silent market. Lessons for the future: speech may become a lethal weapon, when it is used for calumny; if left unbalanced, the exchange may become frustrating and therefore dangerous.

Twenty thousand years ago, the most advanced of these last primates, who still lead nomadic lives, settle in the Middle East, whose climate is now particularly hospitable. They find, in great abundance and growing in nature, all kinds of storable goods (flax, wheat, barley, peas, and lentils) and animals to capture (dogs, sheep, hogs, cows, horses). Some groups now settle for considerable periods in places where they build the first stone houses. The sacred accompanies them, and certain gods are allotted plots of land.

Fifteen thousand years ago, these still nomadic men of Mesopotamia dig wells and hold sway over flocks of wild animals they have not yet tamed: they attach increasing importance to succeeding generations, and to a certain extent seek to husband nature as an expression of the gods.

Ten thousand years ago, in order to hunt game swifter than himself, man invents two revolutionary instruments that allow him for the first time to increase his own strength: the spearthrowing stick (his first lever), and the bow (his first motor).

At this same time, in Mesopotamia, men are more and more able to distinguish between an act and its consequences. They learn to water their plots, to promote the reproduction of captive animal species, to reuse seeds, to stock reserves in silos. This requires communal living at fixed sites. And since these men are beginning to live a little longer, they also enjoy a little more time to pass on their knowledge. Cosmogonies grow more complex, with an increasing focus on land and farming. Gods required for travel are relegated to a lower level. And thus, 150,000 years since his appearance, *Homo sapiens sapiens* invents sedentary living. The sacred tips over into glorification of the ownership of land: the gods are masters of both earth and sky.

A thousand years later (some nine thousand years ago), our Mesopotamian begins through progressive crossings to breed new animal species better adapted to his needs. He also becomes a herder. In China at the same time, another kind of agricultural economy evolves, based on millet, pork, dogs, and poultry.

Sedentarism, or fixed living, is thus a hunter's idea. Farming is a nomadic invention, and herding flocks a peasant practice.

Man discovered the need to take control of his foodstuffs. For the past 50,000 to 100,000 years *Homo sapiens* has possessed the same physical and mental motor skills. But sedentarism is not sufficient unto itself; it has to be combined with something else. For a long time, hunter-gatherers remained sedentary in the north of Eurasia, Japan, and along the Pacific Northwest of what is now Canada and the United States. Their presence there was for the most part due to a ready access to water, plentiful supply of animals, and early efforts at growing crops for food.

The Near East is the precursor of Neolithic Europe. Many of the foodstuffs used in Europe emanate from that region, a zone that stretches from the Sinai to southeastern Turkey. The Neolithic period evolved slowly: the first attempts to grow grain date back to 9,500 years ago. The first signs of domestication appear only a thousand years later. Domestic animals arrive on the scene around 8,000 years ago and communities devoted solely to farming some five hundred years later.

Between 12,000 and 9,000 years ago, in the Near East, men begin to build circular houses surrounded by protective moats or pits, as well as four-sided houses composed of various materials: wood, stone, and molded and dried bricks. On the contrary, in Europe, large Danubian houses, stylistically quite different, arrive roughly 5,500 years ago. Made of wood, they vary from 35 to 130 feet in length.

In the Near East, the earliest Stone Age culture is that of the Natufians (whose name derives from a valley in what is now Israel, the Wadi Natuf), which focuses on the cultivation of wheat and wild barley.

Between 10,000 and 5,000 years ago, various Stone Age entities appear not only in the Near East but also in Mexico, the Andes, China, and New Guinea. Seven thousand years ago, there are many important villages in the Near East that consist of several thousand inhabitants each. Then, a thousand years later, this tendency disappears. The Stone Age at that point in history extends from Turkey through Central Asia and into Europe, where Neolithic techniques disseminate along two routes: the Mediterranean coast and the Danube. Over the next two thousand years the entire European continent will be populated as far as the Atlantic, by which point farmers feel obliged to seek out new ways to increase productivity, and a number of key inventions follow: the wheel, the plow to till hard soil, metallurgy, and the agricultural use of animals.

In Mesopotamia as in Asia, where humankind has become sedentary, progress now comes fast and furious. Central Asian tribes (which we now call Mongols, Indo-Europeans, or Turks) learn to master the horse, the reindeer, and the camel. They also discover the wheel, revolutionizing transport and mobile warfare, and race to conquer the more welcoming plains of Mesopotamia, India, and China.

To meet the threat, the first villages erect barricades. Houses and ramparts are built of stone. Leaders collect the first taxes to raise armies. Although the villages are sedentary by nature, the first states are born to counter these attackers, who are by nature nomadic. The sedentary now need travelers only to sell their wares and defend them in outposts against other nomads. In several places at once, the sedentary also discover copper, which they turn into arrowheads, then mix it with tin to make bronze. Lesson for the future: conflict between nomads and the sedentary is essential to man's acquisition of power and freedom.

Around five thousand years before the common era (BCE), vaster and vaster spaces are taken over under the authority of a single chief in China. Also in China, they probably invent what will become ceramics and the steering oar, and above all they move toward the beginnings of writing. In the north, the Yang Shao culture develops a system of farming founded on millet. In the south, in the maritime provinces of Jiangsu and Zhejiang, they begin to cultivate the rice that originated in the islands of the Pacific.

The Age of Empires

Six thousand years ago, kingdoms regroup villages and tribes scattered over ever-increasing territories. The sacred retreats in the face of military power, the religious evaporates before military force. Here men's labor is forced from them by violence, and "essential knowledge" becomes that which makes it possible to produce an agricultural surplus. Objects no longer possess proper names or personalities: they are artifacts, tools, exchangeable as such. The enslavement of the majority is the condition of freedom for the few. The chief of each kingdom or empire is at once prince, priest, and war leader, master of time and power—Man-God. He alone may leave traces of his death in an identifiable tomb. All others die unrecorded. The concept of an individual is thus born with the ruling prince, and it is under his dictatorial sway that the dream of freedom awakes.

An empire is born when it takes control of a trade or agricultural surplus, allowing it to defend itself and attack other empires. It declines when it no longer accumulates enough of the surplus to guarantee control of strategic routes.

In North China in 2697 BCE (the first more or less accepted date we possess), there reigns the first high prince whose name has come down to us: Huang Di. At the same time, a little farther south, the Long Shan culture is born—villages protected by high packed-earth walls and by the organization of the region into principalities, such as Hao Xiang. They raise beef and mutton, they grow wheat and rye. Disorder within the region is total. This is the period known as the Ten Thousand Kingdoms.

In Egypt at the same time, King Menes (the first Western ruler to leave a written trace) unifies Upper and Lower Egypt and has stone monuments erected to his glory. Other peoples, known as Indo-Europeans and Turks, found civilizations in northern India and in Mesopotamia. Still others (Turks and Mongols) create city-states in Mesopotamia (Ur, Sumer, Nineveh, and Babylon). A new revolutionary invention that appeared somewhat earlier, cuneiform writing, preserves for us one of the first cosmogonies, the Epic of Gilgamesh, a reflection on desire as the motor of history, the matrix of most sacred texts in the region. Simultaneously in India, the Upanishads are written, a monumental new vision of the world and a new ethos built on rejection of desire. The two great visions of the contemporary world are already there, in situ.

In Egypt, in 2400 BCE, the pharaoh Cheops orders construction of the pyramid that still bears his name. Aryans, Mongols, Indo-Europeans (Scythians followed by Samarians), and Turks develop civilizations of the highest refinement in the Mediterranean region, in China, Siberia, Central Asia, and North India, made up of cities, palaces, ramparts, fortresses, works of art, armies, jewelry, ritual ceremonies, and bureaucracies. All are organized around the forced appropriation of the surplus. In China—already the most populated, most active, most mercantile region of the planet—metallurgy enters the field. So do the first decorated tortoiseshells, the source of Chinese writing. In China too, a philosophy of history is developed, dominated by the Yin and Yang and influenced by the five elements and the I Ching's hexagrams. The literature now speaks of a "Yellow Emperor"—whose existence is just as mythical as his dynasty, the Xia.

And now, just like its predecessors, each civilization is toppled by others, which sometimes make determined efforts to erase every trace of what went before.

In 1792 BCE, the Babylonian emperor Hammurabi incorporates traces of his laws in a code that will serve as a foundation for many others following him, just before his empire is laid waste by Hittite invaders. China sees the arrival of the Chang dynasty, which masters architecture and bronze-working, manufactures earthenware sacrificial vessels, and practices divination by interpreting the carapaces of tortoises. Indo-Europeans (Tokharites) bring the chariot to China, thus giving it mastery of Central Asia. In 1674 before our era, Egypt is in decline, invaded by warrior tribes from Asia, the Hyksos, who use horses and war chariots. They create a new pharaonic dynasty.

In America and Africa, many civilizations ignorant of the wheel and the horse disappear as soon as local natural resources are exhausted.

In 1364 BCE, still in Egypt, a strange pharaoh, Amenophis IV (who becomes Akhenaton), briefly rediscovers the idea of a one God. A little later, in 1290 BCE, one of his successors, Ramses II, repulses a Hittite invasion from Mesopotamia and extends his empire over distances never yet dreamed of.

At this point, more than fifty empires coexist on the planet, fighting one another or dying of exhaustion. It is becoming increasingly difficult to control ever more extensive population groups. More slaves, more soldiers, and more physical space are needed. The imperial order itself begins to lose its meaning: force is no longer enough.

At the same time, amid all these empires, a few tribes from Asia settle on the Mediterranean coast and islands. Unlike most people before them — barricaded within their fortresses and bound by the cyclic demands of agriculture — these tribes (Mycenaeans, Phoenicians, and Hebrews) are fond of change, which in one form or another they call "progress." Although they too revere their ancestors, the intermediaries with their gods, although they worship their lands to which they impute divinity, these Mediterraneans swear only by the political and economic rights of the living. Trade and money are their surest weapons, sea and seaports their chief hunting grounds.

Thus, in the very bosom of the imperial order, tiny, marginalized, radically new societies emerge at the origins of the idea of freedom. Here begins what will much later become market democracy, the mercantile order.

+2

A Brief History of Capitalism

If we are to understand the extraordinary surprises the future may hold in store, we must know the essentials of such surprises in the past. They allow us to determine what is possible, what changes, and what is unvarying. Above all, they help us to awareness of history's amazing potential.

On the shores of the Mediterranean twelve centuries before our era, the first markets and the first democracies flower in the narrow interstices between empires. Two thousand years later, they will constitute the mercantile order. We are still there, and will doubtless long remain. Here follow its history and its laws, which are also those of the future.

Although even today the history books show more interest in the fate of ruling princes than that of merchants (and although they prefer to record the rise and fall of empires, which will continue to share the world between them over the next millennia), the essentials of history's march are now played out here — in the birth of an individualist order that sees the rights of man as the loftiest of all ideals. An order that, by ceaselessly violating its own ideal, produces more wealth than anything that has gone before.

At first this order is nothing more than a microscopic parasite living within theological or imperial societies. Then it competes with them, progressively substituting merchants for ruling princes, manufactured products for all other services. Over increasingly vast spaces, deploying technologies increasingly efficient in the practice of violence, injustice, and splendor, it fosters the market and democracy — *market democracy.* Despite a thousand ups and downs that continue to block the vision of many, it gives birth to the mercantile order. It raises the triumphant ideal of freedom for every man, or in any case for those best prepared to conquer it. Over the centuries it purges every institution until, not much later, it turns convulsive.

The Judeo-Greek Ideal: The New and the Beautiful

Around 1300 BCE, the cyclical notion of the world is turned on its head by a few unbelievably inventive Mediterranean peoples — the aforementioned Greeks, Phoenicians, and Hebrews. They share a passion for progress, metaphysics, action, and for the new and beautiful.

The better to defend themselves against their neighbors, the Greeks revolutionize their ships, weapons, pottery, and their cosmogonies. The Phoenicians, settled in Syria and along the Mediterranean coast, create the first alphabet, allowing transcription of their writings into other languages in the interest of less trouble-fraught trade with their neighbors. At exactly the same time a few herders (who call themselves Hebrews in order to affirm their identity) leave Mesopotamia for Canaan, the land promised them by their one and universal God.

For these three peoples, human life comes before anything else. For them, every man is equal to his neighbor (with the exception of slaves and "half-breeds"). Poverty is a curse: the world cries out to be tamed, to be improved, and to be structured until such time as a Savior arrives to change its laws. For the first time, the human future is conceived of as able — as obligated — to be better than the past. For the first time, material enrichment is perceived as a way of drawing nearer to God or the gods. Such is the ideal that takes hold. It will become the ideal of the West, then of the whole mercantile order down to this day — the *Judeo-Greek ideal.*

A century later, around 1200 BCE, the Phoenicians found Tyre, Sidon, Utica, and Gades (Cádiz). The Hebrews leave Canaan for Egypt. In the Peloponnese and Attica, two other peoples from Central Asia (Dorians and Ionians) develop a handful of cities, including Sparta — a farming city employing many slaves — and Athens — a small trading port wholly turned toward the open sea. The Spartans, sedentary peasants, become a military nation out of fear of their own slaves, whereas the Athenian — traders, men of letters, sailors — develop a formidable fleet to fend off their enemies. According to legend, Knossos disappears at the assaults of the Mycenaeans.

Philosophers, interpreters, seamen, physicians, artists, and traders (Greek, Phoenician, and Jewish, but also Mongol, Indian, and Persian) create commercial circuits connecting all the empires of Eurasia. Crossing every border, even during wars, they transmit ideas and products from the Iberian Peninsula to China, where the Chang are now overthrown by the Zhou, the first dynasty whose existence has been historically confirmed and whose chiefs take the title of Tianzi ("Sons of Heaven").

Around 1200 before our era the Jewish people, back from their Egyptian sojourn, elect judges to lead themselves. But in 1000 they finds themselves under serious threat from the Philistines. With death in its heart, they agree to install a monarchy (Saul, then David, then Solomon). They too have been historically validated. In 931 BCE, they split into two kingdoms.

Shortly thereafter, the merchants of Athens assert their rights against the owners of the agricultural hinterland. For their sole benefit, they invent the rudiments of what will become democracy and money.

The first of these dooms dynastic empires. The second makes it possible to express the value of any object by means of a single standard. Both aim to wrest power from the religious and military orders and entrust it to merchants. Slaves, so essential to the former orders, long remain necessary to the smooth functioning of this new order.

The Judeo-Greek ideal grows more precise: freedom is a final objective; respect for a moral code is a condition of survival; wealth is a gift from heaven; poverty is a threat. Individual freedom and the mercantile order will from now on be inseparable, marching in lockstep all the way to the present day.

Around 850 BCE, the Phoenicians refine their alphabet: it is still in use today. Aramaeans settle in Syria, while in Israel next door Amos, Isaiah, and Hosea deliver their prophecies.

A little later (753 BCE), tiny Athens is becoming one of the world's most influential powers, thanks less to its armed forces than to its ideas and artistic achievements. Meanwhile in China, far and away the greatest demographic power of the day, the Zhou tear one other apart during the Warring Kingdoms phase. At the same time, in the central Mediterranean, another village is founded amid universal indifference — Rome.

At the meeting point between Asia and the West, Mesopotamia is now the setting for all invasions and great population movements. In 722, Sargon's Assyrians take Samaria and exile the Jewish people to Assyria, only to be driven from their land in 630 BCE by the Medes, who return the Jews to their homeland.

The course of the next two centuries is dizzying: the ground rules of individualism become clearer still as events with lasting repercussions gather speed. In 594, Solon imposes on the Athenians history's first democratic constitution. In 586, the Babylonian king Nebuchadnezzar destroys Jerusalem and deports the Jewish people yet again — this time to Babylon. In 538, the Persians, newcomers from the mountains, led by their king Cyrus, also head for Mesopotamia's fertile plains. They seize Babylon and send the Jews back to Israel a second time. They then invade the whole region from Mesopotamia to Egypt, putting a permanent end (in 525 BCE) to the two-thousand-year-old Egyptian empire. In the same period, a Chinese man of letters, Lao

Tsu, declares that happiness lies in inaction and that the only true freedom is that which relieves you of dependence on your own desires. A wealthy prince in India, Gautama, refuses to succeed his father on the throne and becomes "the Enlightened One," the Buddha, injecting new life into the ancient Indian doctrine of Hinduism. Shortly afterward in China, another man of letters, Confucius, says that happiness demands respect for good manners, the family, and the traditions of the sociopolitical hierarchy and the Ancients.

Here we face the great turning point of which we are still the heirs and of which the future will long bear the traces — Asia sets out to free man from his desires, while the West seeks to make him free to realize them. The first chooses to view the world as an illusion, the second to make it the only arena for action and happiness. One speaks of the transmigration of souls, the other of their salvation.

In the Mediterranean (where in 510 Rome becomes a republic for a few free citizens), tiny Athens stands up (to universal astonishment) against the assault of the Persian empire's formidable troops — who nevertheless conquer one by one all the Greek cities of Asia Minor. More surprising still: Athens, with Sparta's help, sends the Persian armies flying — and Darius, an admirer of Heraclitus, the greatest Greek philosopher of the day, is defeated at Marathon in 490 BCE. His successor, Xerxes, is crushed ten years later by seaborne Greek guile at Salamis. For the first time, a tiny city resists an empire. It will not be the last.

The small mercantile world, not yet taken seriously, thus proves that it is already inhabited by an inner rage—by a ferocious desire to live free—and that it can defy bigger enemies. And, also for the first time, the West repels invaders from the East. Now the mercantile order excites the interest of many peoples. It gains strength, and its values grow clearer.

While the prophets announce disasters to come in Israel, Pericles, uncontested master of Athens in 444 BCE, turns the Hellenic city into a great military, cultural, and economic power. For twenty years, sculpture, poetry, theater, philosophy, and the democratic ideal flourish there—until, in 431, an absurd war against Sparta leads to a victory in 338 by a western neighbor, Philip, king of Macedon. In 404, Sparta wins its war against Athens.

Universal lesson: when a superpower is attacked by a rival, it is often a third party that carries the day. Another lesson: the conqueror often makes the culture of the conquered his own. One final lesson: power over the world continues to shift westward, even if most of its wealth remains in the East.

After Philip takes control of the Peloponnese, his son Alexander, pupil of Aristotle, dreams obsessively of India. He reaches the subcontinent in 327, leaving it two years later to die in the Persian capital. His empire then splits into three parts—Greece, Persia, and Egypt—whose splendor continues to flicker on. But Greece has had its day.

The wealth remains in the East. In India, countless small Aryan kingdoms blossom. In China, starting in 220 BCE and through eleven years of an astounding reign, the emperor Qing Shi Huang unifies the country by constructing a capital city, Xianyang, standardizing writing and building the Great Wall. He then has himself buried along with four terra-cotta armies. Closer to our own era a new dynasty, the Han, adopts Confucianism, wars against fresh invaders (known as "Xiongnu"), and opens the Silk Road, the first trading link with the Occident.

To the West, Rome becomes heir to the Greeks without ever truly fighting them. It builds a new empire, the first whose core is in the West. Rome sees itself as an imitation of Athens on a larger scale, even adopting Athens's religious pantheon and its political system. Having digested the lessons of Athens's defeat by the Macedonians, and its own humiliation by Brennus's Gallic warriors, Rome equips itself with a very powerful land army. Soon the city controls all of western Europe, North Africa, and the Mediterranean, and probes into northern Europe and the Balkans. In 170, Antiochus IV plunders the Temple in Jerusalem. In 125 BCE, southern Gaul becomes Roman. The Pax Romana is at its height when (in 44 BCE) a general named Julius Caesar returns in triumph from northern Gaul, brings the Senate of the Republic to its knees, forces the admission of representatives of the conquered lands, attempts to have himself proclaimed emperor, and hunts his rivals as far afield as Egypt, whence he returns to be assassinated. In 27 BCE, his successor Octavius becomes Caesar Augustus, Rome's first emperor. Anxious to avoid any spark of rebellion at Rome's frontiers, his successors crush the Egyptian revolt and silence every dissident. Among them are a Jerusalem rabbi named Jesus and other rebellious Jews. Rome finally destroys

Jerusalem and massacres all its Jews yet again. Christianity is born.

During a first council in Jerusalem in the year 48, Christianity (at first the ally of Rome against the Jews before being caught up in the universal orgy of Roman hatred) transforms the message of Judaism — all men are united in Jesus Christ — and carries it to the pagans. And since the promised Messiah has arrived, the Jewish people (who had announced His arrival) no longer have a reason for existing and must join Christianity. The church will be the new chosen people. Poverty and nonviolence will be the only roads to salvation; love is the condition of eternity; creation of wealth is no longer a blessing; progress is no longer of any interest. The Judeo-Greek ideal finds itself seriously compromised.

There now emerges a degree of common thinking among Christian, Roman, Greek, and Jewish thought systems. Love of God is the most precious of values. Only the church — and incidentally the rulers who are its subjects — may accumulate wealth, which is intended solely to help everyone prepare his own salvation.

Through the sole power of its philosophy, Christianity garners an increasing number of believers in the Roman Empire. This should now have led to a retreat by the mercantile order, by freedom and individualism, to the benefit of brotherhood, equality, nonviolence, frugality, and humility. But this does not come to pass. Lesson for the future: no matter how influential, a religious doctrine fails to slow the march of individual freedom. In fact, to this day, no religious or secular power has succeeded in durably slowing its course.

Unlike preceding empires, Rome at this juncture has no rivals, merely enemies. Tribes coming in from the East, eager to benefit from the Mediterranean's wealth and climate, assail it from every quarter.

Rome is therefore obliged to garrison increasingly costly armies on its frontiers. It has to accommodate the multiple languages and beliefs of its soldiers, manage the burdens of logistics, deal with the challenge of meeting the costs. The emperor Marcus Aurelius goes so far as to spend twenty years, from 160 to 180, on the frontiers of the empire.

But all efforts fail. Under the hammer-blows of Germans and Slavs, themselves harassed by Turks and Mongols, Rome retreats and grows weary, and is soon to find rivals in other cities of the empire, such as Byzantium in Asia Minor.

In 284, the emperor Diocletian tries once again to collect for Rome taxes that are now increasingly rejected. In vain. The empire no longer has the means to finance its defense. In 313, the emperor Constantine, striving to regain the support of his people and nobility, grants freedom of worship to the swelling number of Christians through the Edict of Milan. Once again in vain. In 320, Constantine defeats Maxentius and converts. On the death of the emperor Theodosius in 395, the Roman Empire, unmanageable from a single center, permanently splits into two parts with two capitals, Rome and Byzantium (now called Constantinople). The Roman Empire of the East begins. Europe distances itself from Asia.

A host of Indo-European tribes (Goths, Franks, Vandals, Slavs, Alamans, Lombards, Teutons, Huns, and Mongols) together fall on what remains of the Roman

Empire of the West. These invaders dream only of becoming Romans — in fact, Christians and Judeo-Greeks — in their culture and way of life. In 406, nomad hordes cross the Rhine and penetrate the Roman Empire: the Huns push the Visigoths toward Rome, but they pull back within an ace of delivering the deathblow.

Yet the end soon comes. In 476 the last emperor of the West, Romulus Augustulus, is replaced by a Herulian king, Odoacre. The Roman Empire of the West disappears. For the first time, an empire is conquered without leaving a successor. It will not be the last.

Constantinople remains the center of a virtually intact Empire of the East. In the West, by contrast, bishops, princes, and townships organize themselves into small autonomous powers. In 496, like many other Western rulers, Clovis, king of the Franks, is baptized a Christian and detaches himself from the last shreds of the Roman Empire. All Europe, overrun by brigands and wanderers, builds itself around tiny kingdoms, Gallo-Roman villas, and convents — rare protected species.

Meanwhile, in Asia, America, and Africa, other empires crumble when their leaders — as at Palenque in Mexico — fail to compensate for the disappearance of natural resources. Or they survive when a monarch organizes the move from his capital in time — like the abandonment of Amber in Rajasthan, later replaced by Jaipur. Dynasties also succeed one another in China, without managing to reunify a country that has been fragmented since the collapse of the Han dynasty at the beginning of the third century of our era. Only in 618 does the Tang dynasty raise the country's fortunes again. Buddhism now becomes the state religion: the capital, Xi'an, is still far and away the most populous city in the world. The Tang vanish in turn during a chaotic period known as the Five Dynasties and Ten Kingdoms. Throughout the world, empires become more and more fragile and unmanageable.

At the same time, in Arabia, the future Prophet Muhammad flees Mecca for Medina in 622. His message grows harsher, more geared toward conquest. The Koran is slowly elaborated and Islam is born. In less than a century its power, at once religious, political, and military, overturns aging structures just as Christianity had done. By force of arms, it terminates thousand-year-old empires. In less than a century, the soldiers of the Prophet's successors themselves almost constitute a new empire, light-footed, quick-moving, almost nomadic. To finance their armies these first caliphs, based initially in Damascus and then in Baghdad, resort for the first time to bankers—all of them Jewish because they alone are permitted by their religion to deal in money. The soldiers of Islam rapidly overrun the Middle East, Mesopotamia, Egypt, North Africa, and Spain, often forcibly converting their peoples, before being stopped in France (at Poitiers in 732) by Frankish troops.

The Muslim empire, the Caliphate, structures itself around new lightweight institutions, more effective than those of earlier empires, all of whose knowledge and wealth they exploit. Now (with China) it becomes one of the two strongest powers in the world, and the Caliphate installs its capitals in Baghdad and Córdoba. There all products, all religions, and the whole corpus of knowledge coexist uneasily, their relations marked by sporadic conflict. Highways become safer. The markets of Europe and Asia come back to life again. Merchants, financiers, men of letters, musicians, poets, and soldiers move back and forth from city to city, from fair to fair.

Fairs, Cities, and Nations

Farther north, in the former Roman Empire of the West, the first city fairs of Christianity emerge in the ninth century, replicating those of Islam. Embryonic states appear around them. In 800 the Roman Empire of the West, more shadow than reality, is reborn in Germany, first of all with Charlemagne and then his sons Otto and Friedrich. Close by, two nations, France (dominated by the Franks) and Russia (by the Norsemen), are born, along with countless principalities dominated by the Visigoths in Spain, by the Saxons in Germany and Flanders, and by the Lombards in Italy.

This history is still ours. Even today, France, Russia, Italy, Spain, and England bear the name of one of their invaders during this period. Germany evokes the name of three of them, depending on the language in which the country is named. And Vikings, nomads from the North, are among the founders of the Danish, Swedish, French, Icelandic, English, Russian, and Italian peoples.

In southern China, in 960, unity is restored by the Song and consolidated by the Jin, whose response results chiefly from military pressure exerted by the principalities of the north.

In the Mediterranean, Islam is still at the leading edge of what will become the mercantile order. In the

Córdoban capital of the Caliphate, the biggest city in Europe, they speak Arabic, think in Greek, and pray in Latin, Arabic, and Hebrew. Riches stream in from everywhere—African gold, Asian spices, and wheat from the rest of Europe. There are more books in the caliph's library than in all the European libraries put together.

The other great world empire, the Chinese, controls all the seas of Asia, arranging for the shipment of spices to Europe in exchange for agricultural and craft products, borne aboard awe-inspiring vessels equipped with steering oars and compasses.

Midway through the twelfth century, European Islam is still the first-ranking power in the Mediterranean. In Córdoba, capital of a Muslim empire extending from Andalusia to Libya, an outstanding creative elite comes together: bankers, poets, scientists, merchants, from Omar Khayyam to Ibn Gabirol, from Maimonides to Averroes. In the Mediterranean, Muslim armies and fleets begin to confront the Christian princes' new forces, embarked on a crusade to recover the Holy Places and open a commercial road to Asia.

In the mid-twelfth century, the biggest city in Asia is still Xi'an. Paris, capital of the most populous kingdom in Europe, plays only a marginal economic and cultural role. The most powerful city in Europe is still Córdoba.

Until, in 1148, the Almohades (doctors of religion from the Moroccan south) forbid Muslims to study Greek thought and expel Jews and Christians from their empire. Meanwhile, on the other side of the Mediterranean, other Muslim leaders leave for the recapture of the Holy Places recently seized by the Crusaders.

At this pivotal moment, Islam triumphs in Asia but loses the means for victory in Europe. By shutting itself off from knowledge it loses all chance of maintaining its leading role in the mercantile order. Islam enters into decline, as does China.

The world thus changes radically. The two great empires, China and the Muslim world, turn their backs on the competition imposed by the mercantile order. India, divided into too many brilliant kingdoms, does not concern itself with the rest of the world, except to trade with it for the wealth necessary to the splendor of a handful of princes. Threatened by Islam, Byzantium is no longer agile or powerful enough to become a truly great mercantile power.

These mid-twelfth-century events weigh very heavily on our present, and even more heavily, as we shall see, on our future.

The center of world power now tilts toward Christian Europe, but without fixing on a single one of the great kingdoms in process of formation. France, England, and Russia still lie under the feudal system. Unpaid labor, voluntary or forced, still represents the bedrock of production, and the nobility maintains itself in power by protecting its serfs against everything that moves — mercenaries, brigands, traders, sailors, doctors, musicians, troubadours, explorers, philosophers, and beggars. Even in France, by far the most populous and promising of the three, empire prevails: the sea is not the final horizon, the merchant is not the master. The land still dominates.

Yet in a handful of the continent's rare fairs the new order (still laughably small, parasitic, unseen but revolutionary) pries its way into the narrow cracks between these kingdoms. The mercantile order is still here today, more powerful than ever, and without doubt it is here for a very long time.

In these first townships, men can think more freely than elsewhere. In them, religious and military powers gradually lose control of the economy and of politics. A new ruling class, composed of merchants and financiers, brandishes its freedoms as an absolute ideal. This new class exploits slaves, peasants, wage-earners, and craftsmen, using control of work tools as the instrument of its power. The new elite also forges an alliance with the church, whose misgivings about the financial world wane — at the same time as its restrictions on sexuality are on the rise.

These mercantile elites now elaborate on the Judeo-Greek ideal, establishing freedom to travel, create, transmit, learn, and make a fortune. Bypassing Christian apologia for poverty, they employ a marginally freer labor force — wage-earners — in their workshops and their warehouses, on their ships or in their banks. These elites are neither peaceful nor liberal, for the market needs a powerful state to inaugurate and defend property rights. Mercenaries fight for the merchants' rights and interests. This leads them to delegate management of their common affairs to representatives of their own group, some assigned to creating law, others to implementing it, with the former sometimes keeping a watchful eye on the latter.

In private life, the freedom of each member of the new elite is henceforth limited only to what he owns. In public life, it is determined by the majority decision of the others. All are convinced that these simultaneous decisions lead to their maximum collective satisfaction.

Freedom, mercantile and political, is more than ever the driving force of history.

From One Core to Another

Unlike the two previous orders — in which at any moment on earth a thousand tribes, kingdoms, and empires coexisted, revering a thousand leaders, worshiping a thousand gods, speaking a thousand languages, ignorant of one another or else engaging in bloody combat, the mercantile order speaks a single language, that of money. It constantly reinvents itself in a unique shape, around a single center, a single core, which attracts an *innovative class* (shipbuilders, manufacturers, traders, technicians, and financiers) marked by its taste for the new and its passion for discovery. Until a crisis, or a war, leads to replacement of one core by another.

This springs from the very nature of the new order. Markets and democracy are founded on the organization of competition, resulting in insistence on the new and in the selection of an elite. Moreover, in the very long term, accumulation of capital cannot be pursued in a firm or a family, both of which are fragile units. It is pursued in a city, a core that becomes the organizing center of capitalism. Finally, competition implies battle, and there will therefore be a continuum between market, democracy, and violence.

All cores must necessarily have a vast hinterland for the development of agriculture, and a big port to export their produce. All these cores respond to a lack that otherwise would destroy them; all develop direction from the top in order to gain the upper hand over competition. Emulation, rigor, force, state control, protectionism, and mastery of the exchange rates are their weapons. A city becomes a core if its innovative class is in a better position than anyone else to transform a service into an industrial product. To achieve this, it must master capital, fix prices, gather in the profits, hold wages in check, deploy an army, bankroll explorers, and nurture the ideology that guarantees its power.

Now each core seizes control at home and abroad of the most efficient energy sources and the swiftest means of communication. Bankers, artists, intellectuals, and innovators move in, bringing their money, building palaces and tombs, painting the portraits of the world's new masters, commanding their armies.

Girdling this core is a median zone made up of old and future rivals, either in decline or expanding. I shall call this zone the environs. The kingdoms and empires of the rest of the world, partially governed by the earlier orders, form the outer rim, or what I call the periphery, selling its raw materials and labor force (usually slaves) to the core and environs.

A mercantile form lasts for as long as the core can amass enough wealth to master both the environs and the periphery. It loses momentum and collapses when the core has to devote too many resources to maintaining internal peace or to protecting itself against one or several enemies.

Form by form, each core (bankrupted by its expenditures) yields its place to a rival. In general, this rival is not one of its attackers. It is another power, concerning itself during the core's battles with inaugurating another culture and another growth dynamic, centered around another innovative class, a new freedom, a new source of surpluses, around new energy and information technology, and replacement of an old service by a new mass-produced object.

Form by form, the production of agricultural and later man-made goods is industrialized. Form by form, slaves disappear and paid labor takes their place. Form by form, production of energy and information becomes automated. Form by form, engineers, merchants, bankers, shipbuilders, fighting men, artists, and intellectuals relocate. Form by form, the fields of individual freedom, of the market and of democracy, expand. Form by form, peasants, craftsmen, and independent workers are transformed into insecure wage-earners. Form by form, wealth is concentrated in a shrinking number of hands; wider freedoms are enjoyed by consumers and citizens, and greater alienations are inflicted on the workers.

By a curious irony, this tilt from the imperial to the mercantile order engenders a return of peasant and traveler to a nomadic way of life. Whence the importance of the long history of nomadism (the foundation of human culture), which has resurfaced in our era and which, as we shall see, will be even more present in our future.

Down to our own day, the mercantile order has experienced nine successive forms. We will see that they can be designated by the name of the core city (Bruges, Venice, Antwerp, Genoa, Amsterdam, London, Boston,

New York, Los Angeles). They can also be identified by the roster of services they progressively transform into mass consumer goods (foods, clothing, books, finances, transport, domestic aids, instruments of communication, and forms of entertainment). Or else again by technology that allows men to extend the field of commerce (the stern rudder, the caravel, printing, accounting practices, the reed instrument, the steam engine, the internal combustion engine, the electric motor, the microprocessor), and finally by the name of the dominant currency (groat, ducat, guilder, genovino, florin, pound sterling, dollar). Perhaps even (as we will also see) by the name of an artist or philosopher representative of the core.

The essentials of economic, technical, political, and military history of the last seven centuries can be discerned in the strategies deployed by powers to become the core, to remain the core, to escape the periphery or to exit from the mercantile order. And this history reveals the laws of the future even more clearly than those of the past.

Bruges 1200–1350: The Beginnings of the Mercantile Order

At the end of the twelfth century, a handful of ports in Flanders and Tuscany (whose hinterlands boast the continent's finest farming soil) are home to visiting merchants, rebellious slaves, and serfs driven from their fields. In these townships, on the margins of feudalism, no absolute monarch takes the surplus; serfdom does not monopolize the whole work force; a new innovative class, the bourgeoisie, implements new technical knowledge and economizes on work practices to grasp the profits for itself.

In the surrounding countryside there first appear triennial crop rotation, the horse and ox collar, the windmill, and the mechanization of threshing. These technical advances make possible the beginnings of industrialization of farm products. Then comes the all-important invention of the stern rudder, allowing ships to sail into the wind and, a little later, to arm themselves for the very first time. Such innovations give these townships — at once seaports, arsenals, and fairs — the means of mastering seaborne trade. In the regions they control, money displaces force, wage-earning displaces serfdom, investment displaces monumental building projects, and trade displaces the police. Division of labor grows more complex; agricultural productivity rises; the price of wheat, now produced in great quantities, sinks; more citizens can consume it and buy woolen clothing colored by new dyes; the first spinning machines appear; the need for credit arises. Tiny Jewish communities, sparsely populated on the European continent for more than thirteen centuries but still the only ones theologically authorized to lend at interest, are obliged (as they were under Islam) to lend to kings, traders, and peasants in exchange for a precarious protection — and to create banking systems. And since the seasons are no longer precise enough instruments to demarcate city time, bells appear on church belfries after six centuries of tolling prayer hours in monastic houses. Time belongs to the new masters.

By the end of the twelfth century, Bruges is the

most dynamic of these little seaports. It is still no more than a large township with a vast farming hinterland. Its merchants already travel by land and by sea to Scotland, England, Germany, Poland, France, and Spain, while some of them creep stage by small stage as far as Persia and India. Its harbor, constantly menaced by silting and constantly dredged, becomes one of the most important ports of call of all the great Flemish fairs. From 1227, Genoese vessels moor there; Venetian ships follow in 1314. Italian traders settle there and exchange steel, wool, glass, and Flemish jewelry for Levantine spices, thus partaking in the spice trade of the Levant, India, and China.

Differences between the standard of living of craftsmen and merchants (the "patricians" who control the city) are considerable; one insurrection is followed by another. In 1302, the craftsmen take the side of the count of Flanders and temporarily triumph over the patricians, who are supported by the king of France. Democratic life expands. Intellectual and artistic life, although still under the control of the church, is a little freer than elsewhere.

At the start of the fourteenth century, Bruges becomes the core of the new order's first form—capitalism. A very small core: in 1340, at the height of its power, the city numbers only thirty-five thousand inhabitants.

In the environs of this core are the fairs of the Hanseatic League, Germany, France, and Italy. On the periphery are those of the rest of Europe, dominated by big landowners. The core and the environs ship wine, linen, money, glass, and jewels to the periphery as well as to neighboring empires. In exchange, they receive wheat, timber, furs, and rye. In the big kingdoms, nobody attaches the slightest importance to the bustle of these cities.

In Asia — still the repository of most of the world's wealth — the imperial merry-go-round continues. The Mongol Genghis Khan and then the Turk Tamerlane build vast kingdoms extending from the Pacific Ocean to the suburbs of Vienna. They rule them in nomad fashion, through force and fear. Demographically and economically, they tower over the world, terrifying Europeans who live in constant fear of seeing their vast forces loom on the horizon.

Then this first structure becomes shaky. Insecurity in Asia slows long-distance trading, and a cooling climate discourages the urge to travel. In 1348, the Great Plague (reaching Europe from Turkey and the Mediterranean) kills one-third of the European population and severs mercantile circuits. The Hanseatic ports and Champagne's fairs are ruined.

Bruges no longer possesses the means to maintain its port, which finally silts up for good. By the end of the fourteenth century, this first core gradually subsides (thanks to its beauty) into the eternity of the work of art. For another century, the city will remain the greatest mercantile power of northern Europe, but it is no longer the core of the mercantile order.

While France and England tear one another apart in a war that will last a century, a new mercantile structure takes shape around a still insignificant city, a new core quite as improbable as the first — Venice.

Venice 1350–1500: The Conquest of the East

Like Bruges in its day, Venice is an isolated port with a huge agricultural hinterland, condemned either to expansion or to nonexistence. As with Bruges, it is out of a lack that its power is born, from defiance that its prestige derives, from insolence that its splendor arises. Lesson for the future: after Venice, all succeeding cores will be the products of catching up.

Venice is now a small town, but it is situated deep in the Adriatic Sea and ideally placed to receive the silver just discovered in German mines. But necessity is not enough: luck also plays a part. Venice encounters the opportunity with the late-eleventh-century Crusades. To build the Crusaders' vessels, financed with money stolen from the Jewish communities massacred en route, the Most Serene Republic constructs shipyards.

Even though the early-thirteenth-century sack of Constantinople by the Crusaders and their departure from Venice briefly interrupt this traffic, the Serenissima remains throughout the century Europe's only shield against the Turkish menace, and an obligatory stopover for Asian products destined for northern Europe. In addition, a daring bridge on the flanks of the Brenner Pass opens the route from Saint-Gothard and directly links the German silver mines to the Adriatic. It allows the cities of the North to receive products from the empires of the East, with no more need to use the threatened Flemish ports nor the arrogant merchant houses of northern Europe. Germany is still just a point of passage, and the North Sea ports, from Altona to Talinn, will never succeed in rising to the status of a core or scarcely even that of environs.

When, midway through the fourteenth century (and after the end of the Great Plague), Bruges suddenly declines, Europe experiences a fresh craving for life and its pleasures. For the next hundred years Venice becomes the core of the mercantile order. Although living in the shadow of the Turks, the city takes control of trade between Europe and the East.

Like Bruges, Venice by now is an entity ruled with an iron hand by princes who are at once merchants and soldiers. The doge (duke), chief of the executive and theoretically elected for life, can be forced to resign under pressure from the oligarchs. For its own account, the city establishes the workshops and financial institutions necessary for shipbuilders, bankers, and merchants, who now pour in from the four corners of the world. Even more than was the case in Bruges, it enjoys a formidable intellectual, artistic, and human freedom. Waging a war never won and never lost against the Roman Empire of the East, and then against the Ottoman Empire, Venetian leaders constantly negotiate skillful compromises, often trading glory for wealth. Meanwhile, the Hundred Years' War exhausts the rest of Europe.

The Chinese empire suffers successive coups d'état, with the Jin dynasty replaced by the Mongols and then, in 1368, by the Ming. In spite of these political upheavals, an unprecedented mastery of farm production and a redoubtable bureaucratic system allow China to implement major technical advances (such as the movable press), to produce more than ten tons of iron each year and to finance a million-man army. Turned once again toward the exterior, the imperial fleet sends exploratory missions led by a certain Zheng He as far afield as Africa, Australia, and perhaps even the Americas, but without gaining control of the trade routes or seeking to conquer markets or spread knowledge. Other empires—Indian, Russian, Mongolian, Turkish, and Greek—still separate China from Europe.

Venice, a very modest city in comparison with these huge empires, now becomes the center of the mercantile world. Venetians set the price of the major commodities, manipulate the rates of their own currency, accumulate profits, and establish aesthetic, architectural, graphic, and musical canons. Writers, philosophers, and architects—of whom Palladio will soon be master—flock in to write and to theorize about freedom before spreading their ideas throughout Europe. The Catholic city distances itself from the Roman Church and rejects all its attempts to moralize. By the end of the fourteenth century, Venice dominates Europe. Venetian money changers control all the continent's financial markets, from France to Flanders, Castile to Germany. Differences in power are enormous—the Venetian standard of living is fifteen times higher than that of Paris, Madrid, Antwerp, Amsterdam, or London.

Venice is now a complex city, ruled by a narrow aristocracy and several thousand first-class strategists. Under their governance, the hundred thousand guild members, protected wage-earners with high earning power, keep the workshops moving. Below them toil the "proletariat of the sea"—some fifty thousand seafarers subject to the laws of a remorseless labor market. And many others, insecure and evanescent—mercenaries and courtesans, the religious, artists, and physicians.

The city now equips itself with a fleet of three-hundred-ton merchant ships (*galere da mercato*), using both oar and sail power, sturdy and stoutly defended by mercenaries. It leases them to merchant cartels whose position is constantly challenged, for once again military necessity impinges on the demands of commerce.

Like Bruges and other cores to follow, Venice is not the center of technological innovation. The core does not invent—it hunts down, imitates, and implements the ideas of others. This will hold true for all its successors. Thus, at this same moment (while Genoa mints the first gold coin, the genovino, and Florence invents the check and the holding company), Venice is the first to gather them into a sophisticated system of stock exchanges, trading houses, banks, and insurance companies. Venice is also the first to have ships chartered by shareholding companies financed by a great number of small depositors.

The world becomes the locus of adventure for seafarers, discoverers, and explorers, civilizing by the sword in the service of Venice.

And then, around 1450, like the rest of Europe, the Serenissima runs short of money. To find it, like everyone else, it seeks ways of reaching the unknown lands described in legends evoking fabulous kingdoms where gold is to be found in unlimited quantities. Alas, the Venetian sailors return empty-handed.

Threatened neither by France, nor Spain, nor England, Venice now becomes a menace to itself.

Maintaining its structures becomes increasingly costly, and its guilds become more and more rigid. Its galley cartels and its armies are neither big enough nor well enough equipped to defend its routes. The precious metals extracted from German mines are rarer and costlier. Smothered by Turkish pressure, this city of one hundred thousand people has become too rich and too intent on the good life, and is about to grow weary.

This sudden weakness brings down upon Venice enemies that its power had kept at bay. In 1453 the Turks, already masters of almost the whole of the old Empire of the East, take Byzantium—encircled for a half century—and challenge Venetian domination of the Adriatic. The Empire of the East perishes. A sign of the times: Greeks driven from Byzantium by the Turks seek asylum in Florence and not in Venice. The Serenissima has lived out its time.

Which city can now become the third core?

Florence cannot, because it is not a port. And the port it uses to ship its magnificent fabrics, Genoa, is not yet ready to pick up the torch from the Most Serene Republic. Bruges might return to power. The city is still powerful, attracting both artists and merchants. Jan van Eyck paints the first portrait of merchants in the history of painting—two Florentines settled in Bruges, the Arnolfini, thus signaling the entry into art history of the secular individual. But in 1482 the Flemish city's splendor fades forever with the death of Marie of Burgundy, which puts an end to the Burgundian splendor on which Bruges depended.

At the same time, Ming China forbids its subjects to build oceangoing vessels or to leave the country. The planet's leading power decides yet again to avert its eyes from abroad. In so doing it cuts itself off all over again — and the rupture will endure for a considerable length of time — from the mercantile order.

No port in France, England, or Russia yet possesses the means to take over from Venice. In those countries the rulers spend recklessly, building monuments and exhausting themselves in fruitless warfare, while their bureaucracies wear themselves out trying to curb their expenses.

It is now that the caravel enters the picture: an outer jib, two square sails, and a lateen make of it a totally mobile vessel. Perfected in Portugal around 1430, it might have handed power to Portugal's navigating rulers, ideally situated to explore the African coastline and link Flanders to the Mediterranean. But Prince Henry the Navigator and his successors are more eager for glory and salvation than for commerce.

Seville might also have become the third core. Castile and Aragon, now united under a single crown, are ideally situated to range over all the seas, from Flanders to the eastern Mediterranean. When the Genoese Christopher Columbus, seeking gold for the Spanish kings, stumbles upon a new continent full of promise, he might still have been able to make Spain the world's premier power and Seville the new core of the mercantile order. But the Andalusian port (with its southerly neighbor Cadiz) lacks an agricultural hinterland, confidence in its own bankers, and the expert shipbuilders it needs. The city places too much trust in its military commanders. The Most Catholic Kings and their court think only of consuming, idly and unproductively, what they steal in the Americas while slaughtering the natives. They foster no technology, no industry, no commercial networks. Worse: by expelling Spain's Jews and Moriscos they discourage their own innovative classes, leaving the core to two ports in succession, ports which through the workings of dynastic chance have become at once provinces of the Hapsburg Empire and Spanish colonies—Antwerp, followed by Genoa.

Around 1500, one after another, these two cities will don the mantle of Venice after a century and half of the Serenissima's reign. The cores of two short-lived forms, they share the sixteenth century between them. Lesson for the future: accessibility to foreign elites is one of the conditions of success.

Antwerp 1500–1560: The Triumph of the Printing Press

First, around 1500, comes Antwerp's day. Blessed with a rich hinterland where farmers raise the sheep that provide the wool Antwerp spins, over the past two centuries the city has traded Flemish linen, Zeeland salt, English cutlery, Flemish glassware, and German metals for products from the East. It still has only twenty thousand inhabitants when (around 1450) it becomes the Low Countries' principal port. There, northern European products are traded for the spices now arriving from Africa and Asia aboard Portuguese and Spanish ships: pepper, *malagueta*, cinnamon, and sugar. Everyone, even the French and English, comes here to have fabrics dyed using techniques the city jealously keeps secret.

The Antwerp Exchange becomes Europe's leading financial center for insurance, wagers, and lotteries. The city builds a sophisticated banking network, using new silver currencies — their rates strictly controlled — such as the groat, to finance external trade. Lacking an army, Antwerp dominates the form — as the other cores have already done and will continue to do — through its ability to manage the financial markets and dragoon them into its service. Lesson for the future: closely linked, finance and insurance make up an essential dimension of commercial power.

Antwerp is also (as other cores will be) the first industrial user of a major technological innovation from abroad: the movable-type printing press, a Chinese invention rediscovered in Germany and at first reserved exclusively for the church.

What we have here is the first in a long series of advances aimed at accelerating the transmission of data. The written word becomes the major source of wealth, whose marginal reproduction cost is virtually zero. It will not be the last. The book thus becomes the first mass-produced nomadic object. It too will not be the last.

The success of the printing press is dazzling, so hungry are the new administrative classes for the things they favor — freedom of expression, the progress of individualism and of reason, and the wider dissemination of the Judeo-Greek ideal.

Around 1490 (forty years after their arrival in Europe), presses are at work in 110 European cities. At first, Venice leads the way, then Antwerp plays a key role with the workshops of Christophe Plantin. By 1500, twenty million texts have already been printed in

Europe. In Florence, the books of Marsilio Ficino and Pico della Mirandola lead to a rediscovery of the Judeo-Greek and Arabic heritage — hitherto painstakingly censored by the church. New readers now find that the Bible does not offer exactly what the priests say of it, that it also contains philosophical essays and even novels, that it speaks of reason and love, and that a corpus of knowledge (Jewish, Greek, Roman, Arabic, Persian) has been carefully sealed off from them. Many wish to read these texts in another language than the Latin they no longer speak. Vernacular tongues batter at the language of the church so effectively that Latin is soon just the official language of a handful of chanceries.

In all, in the space of a few decades, the press shatters the dream — long cherished by the Vatican and the Holy Roman Empire — of homogenizing Europe around the Latin language and the church. Lesson for the future: a new communications technology, seen as a centralizing influence, turns out to be the implacable enemy of the powers that be.

In 1517, Luther has his followers read the Bible, rebels against the corruption of the papacy, and joins forces with the German princes against church and emperor. Protestantism now places itself at the service of nationalism and builds its nest there. The era of nations can begin.

Sovereign in Madrid and Flanders, Charles V must now confront the clamor for independence coming from the Low Countries. Those claims are supported by England (Protestant like the Low Countries). He vainly seeks to make Antwerp off-limits to the foreigners who continue to flock there, accelerating progress and the city's forward march. The leading German bankers — the Höschstellers, Fuggers, and Welsers — descend upon it. Silver from the Americas arrives by the shipload, and it is on silver that the city's trade is henceforward based. At its apogee in 1550, Antwerp numbers one hundred thousand inhabitants. Cores are getting bigger.

Then this third form of the mercantile order weakens. Like its two predecessors, it once again loses the means of holding its networks together. Massive exploitation of America's silver mines lowers the value of the metal underpinning Antwerp's commercial networks. Trading in gold, now costlier and out of Antwerp's control, becomes much more tempting to speculators. What is more, the Wars of Religion disrupt seaborne links between the Low Countries and Spain, and sever Antwerp (which lacks a standing army) from its commercial networks. American silver can no longer head northward, but must either remain in Seville or be shipped to the Mediterranean. In 1550 Antwerp, now at the mercy of the slightest financial crisis, is forced to step aside, broken by share speculation that originates in Seville.

France, the biggest and most populous European nation, now has a second chance of becoming the core of capitalism. Its standard of living soars and its navy improves. In 1524, Giovanni da Verrazano, a Genoese turned Frenchman, ships out from Honfleur under the orders of François I and is the first to enter New York Harbor. But France, lacking a sturdy middle class, a merchant fleet, and a large port either in the Mediterranean or on the North Sea, fails to raise itself to the status of a core. Moreover, its size plays against France:

its domestic market is so enormous that it has no need to export the products of its industry and agriculture, nor even to export products with high returns.

Elsewhere, in Germany and Poland, the feudal system and serfdom linger on. The nobility, fearful of the rise of its domestic middle classes, satisfy themselves with admitting a handful of foreign merchants who come in to purchase wheat for the rest of Europe. Finally, despite the fascinating trading dynamic of a few Baltic ports, northern Europe remains marginal.

Spain too has a second chance of raising itself to the top rung. First the silver and then the gold of the Americas guarantee it an immense income that might help it finally become a core. But the imperial culture is more influential than ever; lords dominate merchants; Spanish soldiers receive increasingly high wages, although Spain does not produce the textiles, jewelry, and weapons they dream of. It must therefore import them from the Low Countries and Italy. Inflation sets in, Castile sinks into debt, its currency is eroded, bankers quit the financial centers of Madrid and Seville, which go bankrupt in 1557. Next, in 1560, it is Lisbon's turn to founder.

Antwerp is dragged down by the Spanish collapse. The Atlantic is no longer secure enough to carry the world's traffic.

Genoa 1560–1620: The Art of Speculation

The only available Mediterranean port, Genoa (site of the foremost gold market), becomes the new heartland around 1560. It will last for just over a half century, as though the mercantile order still hesitated to leave a Mediterranean that had witnessed its birth.

As early as the thirteenth century, Genoese businessmen had realized that political power was a fount of troubles. To exercise that power, they find two families, the Viscontis and the Sforzas, and devote their energies to trade and finance. In the fourteenth century, that is to say as soon as the church authorizes them, certain of these Lombards become financiers and finally issue interest-bearing loans. Among them are many converted Jews. These bankers first finance — in silver and gold — most of Europe's rulers, and later the bulk of Florentine trade and its textile industry.

Their power is based on their remarkable accounting abilities. For Genoa, in fact, accounting is what the printing press represented for Antwerp or the *galere da mercato* for Venice — a major strategic innovation that guarantees its power over all other mercantile networks. It is also in Genoa that first Patini and then Masari invent the profit-and-loss system of accounting. Thanks to the works of the Genoese Luca Pacioli, it later spreads abroad. This is a revolution in the economic and philosophical orders.

For accounting, like philosophy, is also the art of weighing the negative against the positive; and reason makes strides in Genoa around the figure of the merchant who takes risks, who speculates on the future, and must therefore attempt to foresee it. In Genoa as elsewhere, this innovative class is now particularly influenced by the writings of Jewish exiles from Spain, such as Isaac Abravanel, and by the works of Jean Bodin, the first

Frenchman to speculate on the concept of sovereignty and make himself a spokesman for religious tolerance.

Falling under Spanish domination early in the sixteenth century, Genoa thus becomes Europe's leading financial market, the core of the capitalism of its day. Masters of the gold trade, Genoese bankers fix the exchange rates of all currencies and finance the operations of the kings of Spain and France, as well as those of the Italian, German, and Polish princes.

Since no port can become a core without also controlling farming and industry, the Genoese hinterland (which extends far beyond fabulously wealthy Tuscany) becomes a great industrial, wool-producing, and metallurgical power. Genoa now generates the Mediterranean world's final explosion of energy—the last echo of the dream of Athens, Rome, Florence, and the Spanish kings Charles V and Philip II.

Then the Atlantic becomes a peaceful ocean once again. In 1579—eight years after the meaningless victory at Lepanto of Charles V's unacknowledged son over Selim II's Turks—the Spanish are driven from the Low Countries, an event much more consequential and less celebrated than Lepanto. The English fleet, a newcomer on the seas, led by great captains like Francis Drake and Thomas Cavendish, arrives to steal the gold still flowing in from the Americas. In 1588, the invincible Spanish Armada, cumbersome and ill-manned, founders off the coast of England. Two-thirds of its seamen and ships sink while confronting English vessels armed with much more accurate cannon. Now the Atlantic is open once again to merchant shipping, and in particular Genoese, Dutch, English, and French vessels. It becomes a new locus of commerce.

While China defeats the Japanese in Korea in 1598 without actually occupying the peninsula (this will happen again on three occasions and will fix essential ground rules for the future), Genoa grows weary. The city no longer boasts sufficient human and financial resources to stand up to its rivals on every front. Without an army, the city cannot prevent the Dutch — free at last — from taking control of the new Atlantic seaways and welcoming the American gold and silver which Antwerp had vainly lusted for a century earlier. But like Antwerp before it, Genoa is now enfeebled by a new countrywide recession in Spain.

Born after a stock exchange coup of the kind that weakened Antwerp, Genoa fades away around 1620, following a power move that strengthens Amsterdam. And with Genoa, the Mediterranean fades forever from the front rank.

Around 1620, capitalism's center tilts a second time from Mediterranean to Atlantic. There will be no going back: the Mediterranean forever becomes a secondary body of water. The countries surrounding it — the kingdom of Spain, Italian principalities, southern France — fall into decline, even permanently losing contact with the core. Henceforth their standard of living will always be inferior to that of the new powers.

The Low Countries have enormously lengthened their lead. Their living standards have overtaken those of Genoa and Venice. They are five times higher than those of France, Spain, and England.

The same logic still prevails—progressive expansion of the mercantile space, of industry's reach, of finance and technology. This logic raises a new innovative class to power, at once interventionist and free, in a modern port blessed with a vast agricultural hinterland, a shipbuilding industry, a battle fleet and a merchant fleet, its arms open to financiers, shipbuilders, innovators, and adventurers. Little by little, this logic extends the rights of wage-earners and condemns forced labor to extinction. It takes global control of raw-material sources and of markets.

For nearly four centuries, the Atlantic thus becomes the most important sea in the world.

Amsterdam 1620–1788: The Knack of the Flyboat

After Antwerp and Genoa, Amsterdam rebuilds the networks essential to a core. To pay for its imported food, Amsterdam's backcountry produces sophisticated agricultural goods (flax, hemp, rape, hops), raises sheep, and develops the dyeing industry and the mechanization of spinning. This permits it to begin industrialization of garment production after the industrialization of food production. Amsterdam dyes fabric of virgin wool for the whole of Europe. This includes England, despite London's protectionist measures. With its resulting surpluses, the city can begin to industrialize the construction of an exceptional vessel, the flyboat—much more economical than its predecessors for it can be mass-produced and requires only four-fifths the number of seamen.

In the early seventeenth century, Amsterdam turns into an immense site for the production, sale, and maintenance of ships. Its workshops use cranes and wind-powered saws. Its fleet is now enormous, extraordinarily well manned and armed, and beyond comparison with the fleets of any other country. The Dutch operate two-thousand-ton vessels, with a crew of eight hundred, transport cargoes six times bigger than all the other European fleets combined—in other words, three-quarters of the grain, salt, and timber and half the metals and textiles of all Europe. And since war always supports trade, the Dutch navy becomes master of the seas from the Baltic to Latin America. The Dutch East India Company, and later the Stock Exchange and Bank of Amsterdam, now turn this naval power into an instrument of financial and commercial domination. It is also Amsterdam that dreams up the financing of land-bound operations by stockholding companies in 1604.

Like its predecessors, this new format replaces new services with industrial products and new forced laborers with wage-earners. It increasingly concentrates the wealth in a decreasing number of hands, and grants greater freedoms to its citizens and to consumers while inflicting increasing alienation on its workers.

This fifth core is no longer just a city: it is now a whole region. Leiden is its industrial center, while Rotterdam focuses on shipbuilding. Amsterdam's bourgeois regents dominate the province and control the surplus, despite conflict between the Great Pensioner of Holland and the Stadhouder of the United Provinces. Even though slavery has entirely disappeared, the people work hard and are often hungry. Protestantism also liberates men from any guilt in regard to wealth: the church is no longer there to monopolize fortunes. Public life is sumptuous, intellectual life intense; famous universities welcome foreigners. Around 1650, one of their descendants, Baruch Spinoza, has the audacity to imagine a world in which God would be lumped together with Nature, without attempting to impose a moral code on men resolutely autonomous and free.

The rest of the world gazes, fascinated, at this triumph (it will last nearly two centuries and will be the longest-lived mercantile form of all time).

Yet when they describe this period, our history books still dwell longer on the fate of monarchs than on that of wealth. In 1644, the Middle Kingdom is still the world's leading economic power when Manchu nomads overthrow the Ming dynasty and found the Qing, its capital now in Beijing. The Qing will remain in power for two and a half centuries. In France in 1643, Louis XIV ascends the throne and in 1648 puts an end to the Thirty Years' War that has devastated Europe. But despite his apparent splendor, the Sun King lacks the means to rival the United Provinces. By 1685 (date of the revocation of the Edict of Nantes), the per capita income of Amsterdam's inhabitants is already four times higher than that of Parisians—and the gap widens still further with the departure from France of its Protestant Huguenots.

The world is changing. Bruges is now just a second-rank city, Antwerp a suburb of Amsterdam; Genoa is in decline: along with the rest of the rest of Lombardy, it is gradually excluded from the major mercantile circuits. Venice is no more than a sumptuous chapter in the history of trade with the East. Spain remains sealed off behind the Pyrenees. China timidly raises its head: in 1683 the emperor occupies Taiwan. New powers emerge: Austria rises to become a rampart against the Turks; in 1689 Peter the Great's Russia becomes an international player. Prussia does the same in 1740 under Friedrich von Hohenzollern. In 1720, Qing China takes Tibet and then the Altai region (modern Xinjiang) — a Muslim zone. All this time seventeen million Africans, sold as slaves by Arab traders, have been deported to various European colonies by Portuguese, Spaniards, Dutchmen, Englishmen, and Frenchmen. As it has done since the inauguration of the mercantile order, the science of geopolitics develops more fruitfully alongside trade and industry than dynasties.

For the Low Countries, the eighteenth is still a triumphant century — and for its rivals a time of repeated failure. With its small population (about three hundred thousand inhabitants), it runs European politics with a masterly hand. Its navy controls all the seas; its bankers reign over exchange rates; its merchants fix the price of all products. Despite its apparent power, France — Europe's most populous country — endures check after check: military failure at sea, diplomatic failure in the Indies, Louisiana, and Canada, financial failure with the bankruptcy of the speculator John Law. Although by 1714 it finally becomes possible for the French aristocracy to engage in trade without demeaning itself, the tiny French bourgeoisie interests itself neither in its navy nor in modern industry. France's economy is content to vegetate in the outmoded industries of agricultural capitalism (food, leather, wool) that the daring merchants of the United Provinces are only too happy to leave in its hands.

All this time in China, where the practice of three annual rice harvests permits the population to expand from 180 to 400 million inhabitants (far ahead of any other country on the planet), there is no response from the emperor when Dutch merchants begin to trade in Canton from their Indian Ocean bases.

And yet, around 1775, a century and a half after taking power, this fifth mercantile form declines, like its predecessors and for the same reasons. Dutch warships are no longer the most powerful, the seas are no longer their playground, defense of their commercial routes is increasingly costly, and the energy used by their industries (forest timber, also essential in shipbuilding) is close to exhaustion. Dutch dyeing and shipbuilding techniques no longer make progress; social conflicts are on the rise; wages soar; and Amsterdam's woolen industry is becoming an increasing burden.

Lesson for the future: it may seem eternal, but no empire can last forever.

Elsewhere in Europe, the middle classes murmur and call for greater freedoms—nationalism is now a force to be reckoned with. A premonitory sign that cannot lightly be ignored: the rulers of every European court now insist that their musicians write their opera librettos in their national language and not in Italian, which had been the custom hitherto. Music—harbinger of the future.

In 1776, Britain's colonies in America declare their independence. In 1781, the French navy, in a rare moment of effectiveness, makes it possible for the American insurgents to win the battle of Yorktown. In Europe, hungry peoples cry out. Throughout the continent, war threatens. Shipbuilders, followed by the best Dutch financiers, leave the Low Countries for London, by now Europe's safest and most dynamic city.

As always, a financial crisis confirms the decline of a heartland. In 1788, the Low Countries' banks declare bankruptcy. On the eve of the French Revolution, the core of capitalism crosses the North Sea for good to settle in London, where democracy and market move forward together.

London 1788–1890: The Power of Steam

As early as the sixteenth century, England had mastered wool-spinning, coal-mining, and glassblowing technologies. Its abundant streams, serving primarily as energy sources, foster the mechanization (in Lancashire) of spinning a new raw material for the textile industry, soon to be a rival of wool — cotton, long familiar in Europe and rediscovered by the British in India.

To possess this vegetable fiber, henceforth as strategically important as Peru's gold and silver, the British East India Company assumes control of India, large tracts of North America, and South Asia, all cotton-producing regions. The first English bridgehead in South Asia had been established in 1619 at Surat, on India's northwest coast. A little later the British East India Company — which manages these regions solely in its own interest — sets up permanent trading counters in Madras, Bombay, and Calcutta. British armies do the same in North America. England is now importing from its colonies—at rock-bottom prices—every conceivable product (wool, cotton, silk, leather, tin, tobacco, rice, indigo), which it returns to them—highly priced—in the shape of clothing and precious objects.

In 1689 a political bombshell bursts over London. The country's ruling monarchs, Mary and William of Orange (raised to the throne by Parliament following the execution of their grandfather, Charles I), are back on the throne following Cromwell's dictatorship. They grant Parliament, freely elected by the country's middle classes, the right to look into public affairs. Thus, after its sketchy Dutch beginnings, the birth certificate of modern democracy is officially promulgated. Parliament enacts laws, guarantees individual freedoms, and authorizes the king to raise troops and make war. England is the first market democracy.

That same year, in London, John Locke publishes a *Treatise of Government*, in which he expounds his theory of democratic government, proclaiming individual freedom a natural and inalienable right. Still in the same year, Montesquieu is born in France, where he will later meditate on the separation of powers and political freedom. Henceforth nations will structure themselves around the ideal of equality: disparities, frowned upon by democracy, will remain necessary to the market. The influence of the Judeo-Greek ideal will go on expanding.

In the eighteenth century, Great Britain's wealth increases and projects itself into the world. Its external trade increases sixfold. The share of exports in its national revenue triples, generating a surplus that finances the modernization of its industry and gives birth to a new creative, bourgeois, and industrial class.

As with the preceding cores, this assumption of world power by British merchants is staggeringly single-minded. Following a competition sponsored by Parliament, an English clockmaker-carpenter named John Harrison perfects the first marine chronometer in 1734. It weighs 77.6 pounds. This major invention, willed into being by the political powers, leads to a dramatic shortening of transoceanic voyages. The chronometer thus gives Great Britain mastery of the seas and facilitates a systematic exploitation of the rest of the world. In 1757 the troops of the British East India Company take control of Bengal and force Bengali craftsmen to accept such low prices for their cotton that starvation kills more than ten million people. After three wars with Holland, the English finally take total control of the seas — and in particular, control of the trade in precious metals from the Americas, which the Dutch had wrested from Spain 150 years earlier.

In 1776, the year Adam Smith publishes the first reference book on market economies (*An Inquiry into the Nature and Causes of the Wealth of Nations*), Britain is forced to relinquish sovereignty over part of North America, but it continues to buy vast quantities of cotton from its former colonies in the South until the American Civil War. William Pitt's government restores health to the nation's economic situation by applying Adam Smith's doctrine: in 1786, it even signs a free trade agreement with its archrival, France.

Apparently unchanging, England is in fact in a state

of subterranean turmoil. The countryside is aflame with the vexed question of enclosures; highways become safer thanks to new poor laws; the old elites collapse. A new innovative class, the gentry (landless nobility), takes over the controls, leaving a tiny aristocracy in command of the totality of its landowning income. Every Englishman now pays indirect taxes, whereas in France the *taille*, a direct tax freely translated as "slice," is paid only by the Third Estate.

England now boasts a fighting navy as powerful as France's, despite a population three times smaller, and a per capita income still only equal to a half of its cross-Channel neighbor and one-fifth that of Amsterdam.

As the eighteenth century draws to a close, the bulk of English wool is still dyed in Flanders or the United Provinces. Trade in English products is still under partial Dutch control.

And yet, in the twenty years from 1790 to 1810—with continental Europe wallowing in fire and blood—London takes control of the world. Once again, while one country seeks to overturn another, the market gives power to a third party. Once again, conflict brutally settles a succession widely deemed impossible. Once again, as with the five preceding transformations, this handover of power from one port to another is first of all played out in the countryside.

For the land still supplies all needs: food, clothing, timber for energy and for shipbuilding. The countryside also provides the landowning income that finances industry and generates the first profits. In 1768 Richard Arkwright invents a new spinning machine. Powered by swift-flowing streams, it hoists textile-industry productivity to ever more towering heights.

But energy remains in short supply in England, even more cruelly than in the Netherlands. The few forests it still possesses must be jealously conserved for its strategically crucial shipping activities. And its modest mountains mean that the country lacks the waterfalls that might have met its energy needs.

To find the energy they lack, Britain turns to the technical innovation of a Frenchman, Denis Papin (ignored in Paris because of France's enormous forest resources) — the steam engine. Patented by the Scotsman James Watt, it will first of all help the British extract coal from their soil and use it to feed new spinning machines invented in 1785 by Richard Cartwright. Productivity of cotton spinning rises tenfold in ten years. The concept of the machine now triumphs: in 1812, England actually mandates capital punishment for anyone destroying industrial machinery.

Lesson for the future: scarcity forces men to seek new wealth. Scarcities are a blessing for the ambitious. Second lesson: it does not matter who invents a technology; the important thing is to be situated, culturally and politically, to put it into action.

For once again France could have become Britain's rival. Around 1780, it boasts engineers, markets, advanced techniques, intellectual freedom. But although it harps to the world about liberty, it does not possess a major port, an effective navy, any proclivity for foreign elites, curiosity about industrial machinery. Despite the Enlightenment, France is still dominated by a landowning and bureaucratic caste that monopolizes agricultural income and fails to push it toward innovation. The French monarchy prefers to irritate its British counterpart by supporting one part of its American colonies rather than devote its resources to creating an industry for itself. In 1778, France is already exhausted by its wars, and soon by massive drought, when a financial crisis and then a food crisis burst over Paris.

From 1789 on—zealous in its goal of liberating Europe from its emperors—the French Revolution drives away the country's few merchants. In 1797, as the last of Venice's 120 doges abdicates on the orders of General Bonaparte, the last of France's financiers take ship for London.

Once again, adversity presents the future core with an opportunity. By shutting Britain off from the continental market, the French Revolution incites its merchants to look offshore. Although scarcely more populous than Ireland and almost as poor, this small country throws itself wholeheartedly (like all the cores that have gone before it) into an ambitious project—that of producing for every market in the world with the greatest fleet in the world. Henceforth, London, sheltered from wars, manages most European capital. In twenty years the pound replaces the Dutch florin as the major medium of world trade.

Meanwhile, the new United States of America welcomes millions of immigrants fleeing a war-torn Europe for a land without memory, a land gradually being cleared of its natives—the ideal situation for creating a market democracy, with neither lords nor landowners, entirely at the service of the merchant class.

In 1803, while preparing for the invasion of England, Napoleon sets France on a war economy and sells Louisiana to the United States for fifteen million dollars. In 1804, the emperor rejects an innovation presented to him by an American mechanic, Robert Fulton — the use of steam to move a ship's paddle. He sees no military application for it. In 1807, with the battles of Eylau and Friedland raging in Europe, Fulton returns to America and constructs the first steamship — the *Clermont* — there. The English immediately leap on the invention. In 1814, at the height of their war against a dying French empire, George Stephenson builds the first steam locomotive in London. Irony of history: the world's leading naval power is about to revolutionize land transport.

The end of the Napoleonic Wars reopens the European continent to English products. London is now a huge city, sheltering around a quarter of the country's inhabitants. It is there, in 1815, that the first financial structure (originating in Frankfurt with the Rothschild bank) imposes its market skills and makes possible the financing — through European investment in the steel industry — of English railroads and ironclad ships. In 1821, the first passenger railroad enters service not far from London.

In 1825, for the first time in the world, the industrial added value of a country — Great Britain — outstrips that of its agriculture. (This shift will not take place until 1865 in Prussia, 1869 in the United States, 1875 in France.) At the beginning of the nineteenth century, food consumption represented more than 90 percent of total British consumer spending, but in 1855 it represents only two-thirds — while in the same period the share of clothing doubles.

From 1800 to 1855 the cost price of English cotton is reduced fivefold while their production increases fiftyfold. Cottons, which in 1800 represent a third of English exports, make up one-half in 1855.

But industrial employment remains a marginal activity: in 1855, factory workers represent only the third group — trailing farm labor and domestic employment — of English workers. Although three-quarters of English textile workers are women or children, most Englishwomen earn no wages. They simply look after their homes, thus abetting the relative continuity of the rural lifestyle in the cities. Looking after the home: a major, strategic role — a dead weight on the profitability of the economy, and only partially industrialized a century later.

The core is now so efficient that British taxes can be lowered to the point where they represent only 10 percent of the national revenue in 1860, as compared with one-third forty years earlier.

Like its five predecessors, this sixth form of the mercantile order transforms new services into industrial products and new peasants into poorly paid wage-earners. It concentrates more and more wealth in fewer and fewer hands, procures greater freedoms for consumers and citizens, and imposes further alienation on workers.

The proletarianization of the peasantry, which had begun with England's eighteenth-century enclosures of communal lands, now intensifies. Identity papers see the day, their role the surveillance and supervision of workers and revolutionaries. Jobholders will soon be as dangerous as the unemployed. The working conditions of laborers are worse than those of peasants and craftsmen. In the cities, more than one in three children dies of starvation or disease before the age of five. Among them are three of the six children of a German political refugee, newly arrived in London after the failure of the 1848 revolution — Karl Marx.

Progress is also at work in the speeding up of travel: by 1850, steam begins to replace the sail for transporting travelers, goods, and information. The telegraph speeds up the transmission of the latter. One and the other accelerate globalization, under way since the beginning of the mercantile order. Round-the-world travel is henceforth within reach of armies, traders, and even the earliest tourists.

Democracy progresses alongside the market. In Great Britain, as in France and a few European and American countries, the proportion of middle-class Englishmen with the right to vote gradually increases. Lesson for the future: the authoritarian state creates the market, which in its turn creates democracy,

For the first time, the core of the mercantile order is also the capital of the world's dominant political and military empire. The Low Countries sink. France and Germany wedge themselves into the "middle," to be joined by the United States after the discovery of California's gold mines. From 1857, British armies replace the forces of the East India Company and assume direct control of India. In 1860, they set China afire in order to sell opium there, and acquire Hong Kong and other "concessions." Eight years later Japan — anxious to avoid the same fate — decides to emulate the West and brutally transforms its serfs into urban laborers.

The opening of the Suez Canal in 1869 provides British soldiers (followed by merchants) with a much swifter route to the Orient—where they even more swiftly destroy the Indian textile industry and impose upon India (in the name of free trade and democracy) what is good for British industry.

Like preceding cores, London becomes the meeting place of all the world's innovators, creators, industrialists, explorers, financiers, intellectuals, and artists, from Dickens to Marx, Darwin to Turner.

But London grows weary of its own domination. The country seems first to have taken fright at speed by land: the Locomotive Act of 1865 reduces the authorized speed of trains to two miles per hour in cities and four in the countryside. Much more serious: by liberating the nation's slaves, the American Civil War raises the price of the cotton purchased by the English from America's southern states. London's City, the world's financial center since 1790, is also threatened by the proliferation of new banks in the United States. And the pound is menaced by the dollar. To retain its leading position and maintain profit levels, the English financial world must resort to speculation.

From 1880 onward, Prussian, French, and American rivals are breathing more hotly than ever down England's neck. New technologies and major discoveries fuel stock market speculation in London ("bubble" is the name attached to it), triggering bank failures in the City. Lesson for the future: once again, breakdown in the dominant financial market is the signal for a core's downfall.

For the first time, no European port or nation is in

a position to take the reins from London — even though Prussia has become a great power by uniting the whole of Germany around it, and even if France continues to aspire to that status.

The core continues its westward drift (begun in the thirteenth century) and finally crosses the Atlantic. After its century-long domination, London yields the battlefield to Boston.

Boston 1890–1929: The Heyday of the Machine

The horse gave Central Asia power over Mesopotamia; the stern rudder brought it back to Europe; the galley delivered victory over Bruges to Venice; the printing press was the foundation of Antwerp's triumph; the caravel made possible the discovery of America; the steam engine was the key to London's ascent. A new source of energy (petroleum), a new motor (internal combustion), and a new industrial artifact (the automobile) confer power to the East Coast of America and its then dominant port, Boston.

The means of transport of energy and information, whose mutations have already speeded up the course of history, henceforward appears in the form of a machine, a mass-produced industrial product destined for private use — substitute for the horse, carriage, stagecoach, and even the railroad.

For the third time, France seems to have an opportunity of becoming the core. It possesses in fact an excellent highway network bequeathed by the monarchy. Above all, it is on the cutting edge of technical innovation. It is a Frenchman, Alphonse Beau de Rochas, who invents the self-propelled vehicle equipped with an internal combustion engine.

Yet it is in America that the new core settles. Europe, and especially France, only sees the automobile as an ill-conceived substitute for the carriage. But American settlers — on wheels ever since the conquest of the West began — are obsessed with reducing the duration of their internal migrations. Extreme individualists, entrepreneurs by nature, unable to accept the train, they are best placed to turn the automobile into a product manufactured on a massive scale.

Thus Boston will be the first center of American capitalism.

As early as the seventeenth century, a group of Puritans from England decree that succeeding materially is a way of proving to oneself that one belongs to the elect of God, with rights of entry to paradise. In other words, making a fortune is noble — and it is even morally honorable to boast of one's wealth.

Boston now becomes America's leading port, exporting rum, fish, salt, and tobacco. At the start of the nineteenth century, the northeastern United States is the continent's biggest manufacturing center. Clothing is produced there; leather is worked; machines are produced. It is here too that the fishing industry is concentrated: by 1855, northeasterners are worried about a shortage of oil following the disappearance of the whales. The region now acquires everything needed for a new core — banking in New York, shipping and industry between Boston and Chicago (via Baltimore, Detroit, and Philadelphia). Countless other major innovations, most of them from Europe, are further developed here. They include Thomas Edison's electric light and the gramophone. The telephone, invented by an Italian immigrant, is commercially exploited in the United States in 1877, two years before France.

Unlike all the other potential great powers and all the previous cores, the United States has no credible rival on its own continent. It is thus free to intervene globally, without risk or threat to its territory. It quickly takes control of the whole of Latin America — via the Monroe Doctrine and establishing a long string of puppet governments — and parts of Asia, from the Philippines to Korea.

Here again, this development is perfectly in step with the history of the mercantile order. It spreads wherever a sedentary past does not impede the mobility it demands — wherever a middle class can assume power without decapitating its nobility.

From 1880 onward, a terrible recession, moving in lockstep with England's decline, ravages northern Europe from Iceland to Poland. It triggers the most massive movement of population in history. From 1880 to 1914, fifteen million Europeans (a quarter of the continent's population and a third of the world's savings) migrate to the American continent. A little bit as though, today, over a thirty-five-year period the entire population of France, Belgium, and the Low Countries left Europe.

Following prolonged and violent social conflict, the new American working class wins less niggardly wages, allowing it to buy basic food and textile goods — which as an aftereffect enriches the middle classes, who become customers of the fledgling automobile industry.

Everything will now revolve around this new industry, the instrument of a new individual freedom. And the whole will construct itself around a new Bostonian middle class, so well described by Henry James, and whose values are so perfectly brought to life by Whistler's paintings.

The internal combustion engine is in use in America from 1880 on, twenty-one years after its invention in France (1859). At first it is used primarily for the making of machine tools. Then, around 1890, it is employed in what is to become the automobile, as well as in the first airplanes. North America's first subway is introduced in Boston in 1897. By 1898 there are already fifty automobile manufacturers in the United States. Between 1904 and 1908, a further 241 makes of car see the light of day, including the one created in 1903 by Henry Ford. This engineer, who started out working in Thomas Edison's electric light company, will sell seventeen hundred of them in his first year.

The automobile industry shapes the whole country. At one end of the spectrum it fosters the development of steelworks, mines, oil companies, and glass factories. At the other, it leads to expansion of the highway system, of banks and of trade. It is accompanied by new forms of alienation for assembly-line workers.

Yet French carmakers still dominate the world market in 1907. They produce 25,000 in that year (as many as the United States and ten times more than in England). Two-thirds of cars exported worldwide that year are still French.

Everything changes very brutally between 1908 and 1914. In the United States, assembly-line production of Ford's Model T cuts its price in half. In France, still in love with ancien régime ideals, the automobile industry sees cars as luxury items and designs them like carriages. Thus, when the first mass automobiles (taxicabs) appear in Paris, Louis Renault and his workers, veterans of the horse-drawn carriage trade, refuse to mass-produce them.

In 1914, France produces eleven times fewer automobiles than America, while seven years earlier it built the same number. Ford builds 250,000 vehicles a year and commands almost half of the American market. Britain, bogged down by its empire and unable to control its financial crisis, produces only 34,000 cars, Germany 23,000, and the United States 485,000. Game, set, and match.

The engine of growth is henceforth clearly American, in both the automobile and the oil industries. The world market is now increasingly open, and everywhere democracy gains ground along with the market. In 1912, more than 12 percent of gross industrial production is handled through external trade. One year earlier, the last Chinese dynasty (the Qing) gives way to a republic.

Sometimes this soaring growth creates tension and rivalry over control of the markets and sources of supply. In 1914 a war — seemingly inherited from an earlier time — closes all frontiers. Everything happens as though British, French, and German traders are exhausting themselves in squabbles over a power that no longer belongs to them. Oil shapes the fate of armies and fashions the postwar era. While millions perish in the trenches, the Sykes-Picot Agreement of May 1916 aspires to divide the Middle East (the property of Germany's ally, the Ottoman Empire) between the two great European powers. The United States enters the war following the Zimmermann Telegram, in which the Germans announce their intention to wage all-out submarine warfare; propose that Mexico declare war on the United States in return for the reacquisition of Texas, New Mexico, and Arizona; and urge them to incite Japan to join the side of the Central Powers as well.

By the time it closes with an influenza pandemic and Communist revolutions in Russia and Germany, the First World War has hastened the transfer of power to America, just as the Napoleonic Wars had guaranteed Great Britain's victory. Yet another lesson from history: the victor in any war is the one who does not wage it—or in any case, the one who does not fight on his own territory.

European exhaustion thus reinforces the power of the northeastern United States, from Washington to Chicago, from New York to Boston. Strengthened by the war, the automobile industry triumphs. Now new technologies appear. They include radio and the electric motor. The 1919 Versailles Treaty—its economic clauses essentially written by American financiers—redraws Europe's frontiers. It cuts the Ottoman Empire up into digestible morsels, assents to the creation of the Soviet Union, and burdens defeated Germany with an unbearable debt. All-powerful, the American president can even try to lay down rules designed to avoid war through the creation of a "League of Nations"—first embryo of an illusory world government.

But in America as in Europe, production costs soar, salaries increase, and profitability rates sink: the vision of the future blurs, demand collapses, investments grind to a halt, joblessness bursts its bounds, protective measures harden, and freedom takes a backward step. The creation in 1928 of a cartel of the great oil companies—the "Seven Sisters"—raises the price of gasoline, makes car production collapse, triggers the Great Depression, and puts an end to the seventh form—as the eighth is already poised to take off.

New York 1929–1980: The Triumph of Electricity

As with the seven preceding forms, the birth of an eighth presupposes uniting the cultural, political, and economic conditions for replacing services, whether paid for or free, with new mass-produced machinery. Following the industrialization of farm, clothing, and transport production, it is the electric motor that will now replace—via electric household equipment—the domestic services provided by women in the home or in domestic employment.

As with all prior mutations, the eighth crisis of the mercantile order is resolved even before it flares. Electricity's victory has already been discernible since the turn of the century. Lesson for the future: the time separating an innovation (even one that is socially necessary) from its entry into widespread acceptance always takes something like forty years.

Nikola Tesla's invention in 1889 of the small electric motor first permits the use of this energy source to raise the productivity of earlier machines, which include agricultural and industrial productivity and the automobile. Thanks to Thomas Edison, its second use is lighting: by the end of the nineteenth century, most of America's leading cities are well lit and safer. And in 1906 the federal government takes in hand the creation of a national electric grid.

Then the electric motor permits the building of elevators — and therefore the construction of skyscrapers, a boon to the concept of vertical city planning. The electric motor thus plays an indirect role in rural migration and in the trend toward smaller families. It creates a market for machines capable of replacing a large proportion of domestic chores in apartments steadily shrinking in size. Tasks like cleaning, making preserves and conserving food, cooking, and entertaining other family members are now partially eliminated by mass-produced articles (bathtubs, toilet bowls, washing machines, refrigerators, blenders, radio, and — later — television).

America is particularly well placed to succeed in this migration to its giant cities. Women's magazines and the feminist movement also prepare women, better than elsewhere, to accept their new status as consumers. And advertising, just beginning to spread its wings, ceaselessly reminds them (sometimes in very explicit terms) of what it calls their "special relationship" with the habit of cleanliness. Thus, under the guise of "liberating" women, the market proclaims their servility.

Like its predecessors, this eighth format again transforms farmers and craftsmen into risk-prone wage-earners. It increasingly concentrates more and more wealth into a restricted number of hands. It turns women's lot upside down. It creates greater freedoms for consumers and citizens and fresh hardships for workers.

In 1910, the electric motor first serves to power ventilators and then radios, initially for military purposes. In 1920, the first washing machines and refrigerators appear. By now, half of America's homes are electrified, boasting running water and sometimes gas: the bathroom becomes a major factor in middle-class comfort. At the same time, the Federal Water Power Act looks into the sources of hydraulic energy. In 1921, American industry produces 2.5 million sanitary appliances, doubling that figure in 1925. Production of sanitary appliances, barely slowed by the crash of 1929, reaches 3.5 million in 1941. By 1930, 80 percent of American homes are electrified. Household equipment progressively replaces domestic employees (chiefly black heirs of the recently liberated slaves): their number dwindles from four million in 1920 to 300,000 in 1940, while the rest go to swell the numbers of the jobless. In 1935, Congress passes the Public Utility Holding Act, aiming to give cities access to the low-cost electric power they need to use the new machines.

This eighth restructuring of the mercantile form—this time around the nuclear family—is particularly well suited to American social logic. It also shows up in

Europe, and coincides with the dictatorial upheavals occurring in Italy, Spain, and Germany. Indeed, the family is also at the heart of the Nazi and Fascist ideologies. In 1935, German industrial production is far ahead of that of France, Great Britain, and the United States. From 1933 to 1938, its production of steel, cement, and aluminum triples. But since it needs a workforce, raw materials, and agricultural land, and cannot count on trade alone to acquire them in sufficient quantities, war becomes indispensable to Germany. The Soviet version next door also appears to have succeeded in organizing itself as a war economy—without anyone being able to verify the statistics provided by Soviet propaganda.

The war, yet again willed into being by Germany, once more helps the United States—immune on its own territory—to master the technologies and production levels needed for industry and finance, henceforth based in New York.

Here again, the role of energy is crucial. Hitler marches on Stalingrad to obtain the reserves of the Caucasus (once he has broken the Molotov-Ribbentrop Pact that had guaranteed him the oil essential to his first victories). It is because of the embargo on its oil supplies that Japan attacks Pearl Harbor in December 1941. And finally, it is on his return from the Yalta conference in February 1945 that Roosevelt takes over Saudi Arabia—and the world's biggest petroleum reserves—from Britain.

At the end of this new world war (it cost about fifty million dead—five times more than the first), the world has utterly changed. Nuclear weapons have appeared;

the Holocaust has happened; the Middle East has been splintered into ten sovereign states; communism is triumphant. Now an eighth mercantile form recreates itself in one half of the world (which also includes the former Fascist and Nazi dictatorships), while the other half, from Budapest to Beijing, enters the Soviet orbit. Yesterday's allies become "cold war" foes.

This time, the new mercantile form is structured around New York and electricity. It is the second format whose core is in America. It will not be the last.

From 1945 onward, electrification, family allowances, and housing aid produce a mass demand for household appliances invented in 1920, reviving the world economy much more effectively than major public works.

In the twenty years from 1945 to 1965, and thanks to the electric motor, New York becomes the world's greatest metropolis. The price of household equipment falls fivefold, while production increases by a factor of ten. New consumer appliances intensify the evolution of the market economy in the direction of nomadism (another term for individual freedom). In 1947, the electric battery and the transistor (two key inventions) make radio and record players portable. This is a major revolution, for it allows the young to dance outside the ballrooms and therefore be free of parental supervision —liberating sexuality, opening them to all kinds of music, from jazz to rock, and thus announcing youth's entry into the world of consumption, of desire, and of rebellion. Lesson for the future: the link between technology and sexuality underpins the whole dynamic of the mercantile order.

While the poorest of Americans rise in revolt in the ghettos, the middle class saves instead of consuming. Now the number of people whose profession consists of spurring consumers to spend increases — banking, insurance, advertising, marketing, the media. Between 1954 and 1973, bank loans to American households rise fivefold.

The rest of the world settles into the "middle." While the gross domestic product (GDP) of the United States increases 3 percent per year between 1959 and 1973, Great Britain, France, and Germany (bled white since the Second World War) struggle to make up for lost time, thanks in part to American aid. Japan's GDP progresses from $300 per capita in 1956 to $12,000 in 1980. Outside Europe, the world seems wholly under the control of the United States or the Soviet Union. In 1954, for example, when Iranian prime minister Muhammad Mossadegh nationalizes his country's oil industry, he is immediately overturned in a coup fomented by the CIA: an international consortium, made up of French, Dutch, British, and American companies, takes control of Persian oil production. In 1956, Nikita Khrushchev sends Soviet tanks into Budapest without any reaction from the West. Control is the order of the day.

And now, as in every previous case, the core exhausts itself in military costs abroad and policing costs in its own ghettos. After the Korean War and Vietnam, the U.S. confrontation with the Communist world demonstrates that the capitalist superpower is militarily fallible and financially fragile.

Throughout the West, service activities (whether private or public) cannot yet be automated, and therefore demand an increasing share in the surplus. In the absence of automation of the services provided by white-collar workers in industry, the productivity both of work and of capital stagnates — as military and social spending steadily rises. The profitability of capital declines. Financial circuits direct loans to traditional industries rather than to innovative businesses; toward foreign public lenders rather than private domestic lenders; toward big companies rather than small ones. The steel industry now invests only half of what would be needed for it to compete with Japan and Korea.

In 1973, the rise in raw-material prices, particularly oil, reduces still further the disposable income of wage-earners without raising either production levels or demand. Savings levels sink; debt soars. Inflation follows, reducing the value of the debts and easing the burden of indebtedness, which in its turn spurs and accelerates inflation. The rise in joblessness and the pauperization of part of the population then generate insecurity.

By 1980, the United States seems on the verge of decline; it loses its place as the leading automobile exporter; its share in the world market for machine tools falls from 25 percent in 1950 to 5 percent in 1980 — while that of Japan, a brand-new player, moves from zero to 22 percent. The external debt of the United States rises massively, outstripping its foreign holdings. To finance it, American leaders tolerate the increasing use of the dollar by foreign creditors. New York is no longer the only place where the world's finances are organized. The City of London (where a German emigrant, Simon Warburg, launches the first loans in eurodollars and the first public offering) seems to have recovered a rank it had considered lost forever. Japan becomes the leading creditor for the United States, where it makes spectacular purchases of "iconic" U.S. businesses and real estate. America seems on the verge of becoming nothing more than the breadbasket of a flourishing Japan, just like Poland and Flanders in the eighteenth century.

Many (myself included) then felt that Tokyo might one day aspire to become a new core. Japan possessed the requisite financial strength, a tradition of state intervention, a healthy fear of want, advanced technology, and industrial power. In fact, however, the country swiftly proves incapable of resolving the structural problems of its banking system, of mastering its looming financial bubble, of avoiding a massive reevaluation of its currency, of raising the productivity of its services and the work of its white-collar workers. Above all, it does not attract the elites of the whole world to its shores, nor does it promise the individualism so necessary to the core, nor can it pull away from the orbit of its American conqueror.

It is at this point that a new technological wave gathers force in America, in California much more than anywhere else. This wave in fact makes possible the massive automation of administrative activities in major corporations — in other words a remedy for precisely those ills that had bedeviled the eighth core. It ushers in an extraordinary leap in productivity.

The economic and geopolitical center of the world continues its westward march. Emerging from China five thousand years ago to reappear in Mesopotamia, then in the Mediterranean and North seas, then across the Atlantic, here it is once again on the Pacific shore.

Los Angeles 1980–?: Californian Nomadism

For the ninth time — the last until today — the mercantile order reorganizes itself around a place, a culture, and the financial resources required for a innovative class to transform a technical revolution into a mass commercial market. For the ninth time, this mutation enlarges the space of the mercantile order and that of democracy. It raises still higher the number of the world's market democracies.

This new form, in which we still live today, constitutes the foundation stone of history on the move. We must therefore discuss it in greater detail than its eight predecessors.

Here in California — in this American state roughly the size of Spain geographically, where 36 million people (one American in eight) live, from San Francisco to Los Angeles, from Hollywood to Silicon Valley — the new core takes up residence. This is not a randomly chosen site. Here in the past, men discovered gold mines, and it was here that the oil industry and movies took their first steps, here that the most adventurous Americans gathered, and here that the electronics and aeronautical industries took hold. Here too some of America's finest universities are located, as well as some of its greatest research centers and its best vineyards. California is where the talents of the entertainment industry, the best musicians, and the inventors of all information technologies have flocked. And here too, from its Mexican border to the Canadian frontier, the permanent threat of earthquakes gives rise to an intense, unique vibrancy, a fabulous desire to live, and a passion for the new.

As with all preceding crises of the mercantile order, the technologies needed for the ninth form preexist their use. Because the bureaucratic activities of banks and corporations weigh increasingly heavily on overall productivity, the automation of information and its manipulation become a major factor. First to appear, in the 1920s, are electric machines working with perforated cards. Then, in the forties, the first computers designed for military use rely on the transistor. In 1971, the microprocessor, heir to the transistor, sees the light of day. A tiny chip of silicon piled with thousands, then millions, and then billions of elementary storage and information processing units is put on the market by a new company, Intel, jointly founded by Gordon Moore and Robert Noyce. The microprocessor makes it possible to perfect the serial computer, it too the heir of a long succession of innovations launched in the seventeenth century in France by Blaise Pascal.

From 1973 on, the computer begins to replace perforated cards in offices, leading to a massive surge in the productivity of services and industry. This is the beginning of office automation.

New businesses, Californian for the most part, now make it possible to reduce the costs of services and administration. Most importantly, these technologies make possible an industrialization of financial services, allowing banks to exploit, systematically, the market's smallest imperfections, and to correlate millions of transactions—thus eliminating all limits to the growth of financial instruments and of risk-coverage mechanisms: finance and insurance become industries.

Once again, it is through the industrialization of services—in this case financial and administrative—that a core takes power. Once again (and it is the opposite of what futurologists once predicted), it is no longer a question of the appearance of a service society, of a postindustrial society, but exactly the opposite—these are the beginnings of the industrialization of services, aimed at transforming them into new industrial products.

Like the others before it, this revolution leads to the marketing of new consumer articles. In the new form they play the same part as that of the automobile and household equipment in the two preceding ones. Nomadic articles (a term I coined in 1985, well before such articles appeared, and which has since been assimilated into many languages), miniaturized machines able to receive, store, process, and transmit information—sounds, images, data—at extremely high speeds.

Why "nomadic objects"? As we have seen, nomads have always transported objects likely to help them stay alive while traveling. The first was probably a carved stone, a talisman; then came fire, clothing, tools, weapons, jewelry, relics, musical instruments, horses, papyri. Then it was the turn of the book, the first mass-produced nomadic article, followed by objects promising to miniaturize "sedentary articles" and make them portable: watch, camera, recorder, zoom lens, cassette player. Finally, other objects appear for the processing of information.

In 1976, a newcomer (and also a Californian) creates Apple I, a personal computer that is usable by everyone, with simple interfaces. In 1970 the Japanese market the first nomadic object to sport a quasi-nomadic name — the Walkman, a cassette player invented by a German named Andreas Pavel.

At the same time, a taste for other nomadic objects is emerging — "companion" animals of every species, offering the sedentary an opportunity to live a life of quasi-shepherds, of similinomads, of quasi-horsemen accompanied by a quasi-herd, with none of the risks normally associated with roving, beside a faithful and loyal companion in an ocean of insecurity and disloyalty.

In 1981, as Minitel (an Internet online service) appears in France, the American giant of industrial cybernetics, IBM, also decides to launch its first portable computer, IBM 5150 — but without too much faith in the product. The machine is equipped with an Intel microprocessor, and MS-DOS software produced by another modest West Coast business, Microsoft. It weighs just over twenty-five pounds and is thirty-two thousand times less powerful and twelve times as expensive as the least sophisticated of the 2008 personal computers. Yet it is a triumph — instead of the expected sale of two thousand, IBM sells a million. Ten years later, Microsoft has become one of the world's five biggest corporations. By 2008, 271 million microcomputers have been sold and one billion are in service across the world.

At the same time, two more major instruments of the new nomadism make their appearance: the portable phone and the Internet. They enter the scene just as modestly as the personal computer, but win handsomely as soon as they can interface. For the sedentary, they represent substitutes for traveling; for nomads they are a means of remaining connected among themselves and of connecting with the sedentary. Both offer, for the first time, a nonterritorial address (cell phone number or e-mail address).

The first nonmilitary mobile phone appears in Great Britain at the end of the seventies. At first it requires the allocation of a frequency and a very cumbersome portable battery, until the cellular networks increase their transmission capabilities and the batteries are miniaturized. In thirty years, the cell phone becomes a planetary transmitter of voices and data. Today it is the greatest commercial success of all time. In 2008, more than three billion people—or nearly half of the planet's population—possessed it!

And at the same time it becomes possible to link two computers by phone. In this case too, the globalization of a new technology will take forty years, resulting in the Internet. Its progress is interesting. In August 1962 the Massachusetts Institute of Technology, or MIT, the prestigious university located near Boston, publishes the first articles describing the interactions possible in a network of computers linked by telephone. In 1965 the first long-distance computer connection is tested between a computer situated in Massachusetts and another in California. In 1969, the U.S. Army's nerve centers create the Arpanet in order to exchange electronic information in absolute confidentiality. In 1979, American students create the first newsgroups to communicate civilian data through the hundred or so computers connected in research centers and universities. In 1989, Arpanet arrives in Europe. In the same year, the protocol TCP/IP and the word "Internet" appear. Nineteen eighty-three marks the opening of the first server designed to manage site names. By 1984 more than a thousand computers are connected. In 1989, the Internet opens its doors to the public and the first e-mail addresses are created. In 1990, Tim Berners-Lee, a British researcher working in a European nuclear research center (the Organisation Européenne pour la Recherche Nucléaire, or CERN, in Geneva), invents a common language for all the players connected to this network. He organizes the community of its users, calling it the World Wide Web. On August 6, 1991, he puts the first address (http://info.cern.ch) online.

Lesson for the future: many major innovations result from the work of researchers paid out of public funds to look into something utterly different.

There now emerge very many applications of linked cybernetics, or automats. They too are devised in order to enhance the productivity of services — software for commercial management, for electronic mail, electronic trading, and for the exchange of financial data. By 1992, one million computers are linked, by 1996 ten million, and by 2008 a billion.

The Internet now seems a kind of new continent — this time virtual — to be explored, populated, organized, with a boundless space for commercial activities. Some software businesses join the ranks of the world's great corporations — Microsoft, AOL, Oracle, and Google, most of them now Californian. In 1998, the turnover of the Internet economy surpasses that of telecommunications and of the airline companies. More is to come: the Internet also finds manifold further uses for its portable phone, which progressively becomes video player, camera, television receiver, and blog publisher. In 2004, Apple realizes that profits are built on nomadic objects and not on the data in circulation (usually free of charge)—the iPod replaces the Walkman, once again selling hundreds of millions of copies, just as the iPhone is taking a growing share of the mobile phone market now.

Video games, mingling curiosity and adventure, also evolve, first in the shape of software for solo play, then connected to the Internet to become multiplayer games with an exponential growth rate. In 2008, a hundred million persons play across the network and spend more than a billion dollars on the purchase of virtual property.

In all, by 2008 Internet activity generates more than four trillion dollars throughout the world, in other words 10 percent of global GDP, half of it in the United States.

The Internet also speeds up the development of financial services. As a result, the ratio between financial transactions and the real economy GDP grows enormously, moving in the United States from 2 percent in 1970 to 50 percent in 2008. Also in the United States, international financial transactions represent eighty times the volume of world trade in 2008—against three and a half times in 1997. This means that the annual volume world trade represents only 4.3 days of transactions on the market for currency, titles, and other financial options.

Thanks to the Internet, the insurance market also grows. It speeds up the growth of financial systems by covering the principal risks on the principal markets. By 2008, insurance on property and people represents around 15 percent of GDP in the United States and 7.5 percent of global GDP—around $3.7 trillion versus $2 trillion for energy in 2005. Risk coverage funds are managing about $2.68 trillion by the third quarter of 2008—triple the figure for the year 2000. These funds represent a third of all stock market transactions. They are even beginning to participate actively in businesses listed on the stock exchange, managing the assets of private individuals and no longer those of financial actors. They sometimes take boundless risks and make bets on those risks without enjoying the requisite financing!

The economic and demographic center of the United States now shifts from the Northeast to the Southwest. In 2008, California becomes the leading state in terms of GDP (13 percent of the American GDP for 12 percent of the population), and would rank sixth in the world if it were an independent nation. Between 1980 and 1990, 54.3 percent of national population growth occurs in California, Florida, and Texas. As of 1990, America's South and West account for over half the country's population.

The GDP of the former core, New York State—henceforth the second in size—represents no more than 60 percent of California's.

The United States now rediscovers its dynamic of growth, employment, productivity, and enterprise, a rejuvenation of the pioneer spirit. California's culture of entertainment, from cinema to music and information, finds radically new outlets for nomadic objects. Prices of using other items of equipment, including the automobile, go down in relative terms, and in 2008 the American economy consumes 100 percent less oil per unit produced than in 1985.

The holdings of middle-class Americans also soar. In 2008 they own more than $12.5 trillion invested in real estate and in stock; in the same year, two-thirds of households own their homes (as against 40 percent in 1939). The increased value realized by real estate represent 60 percent of the totality of their gains over the last twenty years. The search for equity, discussed by the philosopher John Rawls, replaces (at least in speeches) the hunt for equality.

More than ever, the United States settles into the role of planetary superpower. It organizes networks and sets up databases to analyze, attract, persuade, and influence.

World economic growth also speeds up, with the mercantile order expanding into new market democracies. In Latin America and Western Europe, dictatorships fall one after another—Greece, Spain, Chile, Argentina, Brazil, and Turkey. As of 1985 the Soviet system itself (which everyone believed to be unshakable) proves incapable of sustaining the arms race launched by the American president and supported by Western Europe. In 1998, when Mikhail Gorbachev attempts to install democracy while maintaining the rules of a planned economy and of collective ownership, he fails. It takes him less than three years to move from glasnost to perestroika, in other words to grasp that democracy cannot exist without a market democracy. The whole Soviet bloc unravels and draws closer to the European Union.

Everywhere, the planetary system moves toward liberalism. By 2008, 137 countries practice more or less free elections; eighty-two of them are virtually democracies — in other words, their executive power is controlled by a parliament, and major human rights are respected there.

The results of this new form of the mercantile order are exceptional. Between 1980 and 2008, world GDP is multiplied by three, trade in industrial products by twenty-five. Planetary production rises above forty trillion euros and increases by more than 4 percent per year, a rate never before achieved in history. From 1985, exports once again represent 13 percent of global GDP, a ratio last reached in 1913.

Power relationships change: in relative terms, the United States stagnates; Europe declines; Asia climbs. Annual growth rates in 2008 are over 6 percent for Asia, much lower in the United States and in Europe as well. From 1980 to 2008, Asia's GDP is multiplied by four, China's by three, India's by three, Europe's by two. Between 1980 and 2008, the U.S.'s share of world GDP remains the same at 21 percent, the European Union's declines from 28 percent to 20 percent, while Asia's (China, Japan, Korea, Taiwan, Singapore, Hong Kong, Malaysia, Thailand, the Philippines, and Indonesia) climbs from 16 to 28 percent.

Although economically united, America, Europe, and other developed nations lose ground: their productivity declines; their competitiveness fades; their dynamism wanes; their populations age. Even though the European Union manages in 1992 to agree on a common currency, it does not become an integrated market democracy; it no longer progresses in step with the rest of the world. In 2008 its per capita GDP is 25 percent lower than that of the United States; its research efforts are much feebler; the best elements of its innovative class leave Europe for the New World; and an important share of the continent's industry leaves for Asia without being replaced by new industries. Russia, although enormously enriched by its immense oil reserves, does not succeed in recreating the foundations for its development. Life expectancy lowers and infrastructures unravel. While social security costs are supposed to represent 20 percent of Russian GDP, in reality they represent only 2 percent of that same GDP. Yet the Russian central bank possesses more than 250 billion reserve dollars.

The Pacific becomes the world's most important body of water. In 1990, transpacific trade already outstrips transatlantic trade by 50 percent: half the world's trade is carried out there. Nine of the world's twelve greatest ports are located on the Asian seaboard of the Pacific, and most airborne freight crosses that ocean.

Once more, Asia is hovering closer to the core. By 2008, two-thirds of Americans qualified in science and engineering are of Asian origin. Even though they then remain for a certain period of time in the United States, many create impressive networks with their Far Eastern partners. Many U.S. businesses (especially in California) are founded and directed by foreigners—eBay by an Iranian, Google by a Russian, Juniper by an Indian.

In 1995, Japan, which as we have seen might once have become the new core, experiences a crisis from which it emerges, much enfeebled, in 2005. Yet in 2008, it is still the world's second-ranking economy.

From 1989, China takes off. By 2008, the world's biggest dictatorship turns out more than half the flagship products of earlier forms (refrigerators, TV sets, washing machines). It is today the world's leading consumer of copper, iron, nickel, lead, and aluminum; the second-biggest consumer of oil (seven million barrels per day, against twenty-one million in the United States and five and a half million in Japan). China even accounts for a third of the world's annual growth in oil consumption. In 2008, China's per capita GDP reaches $2,458 (in Shanghai, it even stands at more than $7,000). In this same year, Chinese higher education turns out 800,000 engineers, and China boasts more subscribers to the Internet than the United States. But Chinese salaries are still a twentieth of America's.

India, which became a market democracy in 1985, also enters a period of strong growth, with an outstanding industrial sector and world-scale businesses. Despite extreme social inequalities (worse even than in China), it already boasts eighty thousand dollar millionaires, and some hundred Indian companies are already valued at more than a billion dollars. In 2008, the Indian agricultural sector still employs more than half of the population and produces only a fourth of GDP. More than 80 percent of these agricultural workers have less than two and a half acres of land. Inequalities among classes, genders, races, and regions are enormous: for example, the inhabitants of the Bihar, Orissa, and Assam regions today are ten times less likely than a resident of New Delhi to one day achieve a higher education degrees or possess a portable phone. And the slums of Bombay shelter more residents than the whole of Norway.

Other Asian countries are also progressing very rapidly. Barely delivered of its dictatorship in 1990, South Korea shoots ahead on all fronts, from the automobile to the telephone. It is particularly ahead of the rest of the world in very high-speed fiber-optic linkages. It is also a multimedia pioneer in partnership with Cyworld, which brings together a third of the country's population, and with OhMyNews, a site for participatory journalism that has become one of the country's most powerful and most widely heard media outlets. Behind the greatest corporations, the *chaebol*, emerge other cutting-edge companies, such as NHN, which develops one of Google's only serious competitors, and NCsoft, which launches one of the leading multiplayer role-playing games on its network Lineage. Korean cultural products sweep in waves over the rest of Asia, earning them the devotion of an audience ranging from Tokyo mothers to Chinese, Vietnamese, and Filipino youth. Korean films, soap operas, and singers make up a "Korean wave" (*hallyu*) that reflects back to Asian youth the image of a society that has succeeded in reconciling Western modernity and traditional Asian values—a model they are more inclined to accept from Korea than from Japan, which has not yet finished the labor of memory over its imperialist past.

By 2008, every Latin American country with the exception of Cuba is a market democracy. In Africa, where dictators are ousted one after the other, some countries are even emerging from recession. From 1986 to 2008, the number of people able to read and write rises, from 42 percent to 67 percent in Rwanda, from 33 percent to 64 percent in Nigeria, from 27 percent to 47 percent in the Côte d'Ivoire, and from 40 percent to 63 percent in Algeria.

Everything thus seems to be in place for this ninth form to reduce poverty on an enormous scale and to last for a very long time.

The Beginning of the End

Yet the end of the ninth form is already looming—just as it loomed for all its predecessors.

First, the mercantile order suffers from many internal contradictions. External deficits explode and their financing is increasingly dependent on foreign sources. While in 1985 the American external deficit (then at 2.8 percent of GDP) was financed at only 8 percent by foreign governments, in 2008 the deficit stands at 5.2 percent of GDP and is financed at 30 percent by foreigners. What is more, two-thirds of global reserves, payable in dollars—two trillion in Asia alone—have lost a third of their euro value since 2002.

Proliferating, excessive, limitless, and out of control, the American financial system requires profitability rates that industry cannot deliver, to the point where industrial corporations now lend their money in the financial sector rather than invest it in their own activities. In consequence, American automobiles, household equipment, television sets, and telephones are no longer of the finest quality on the world market. And American corporations stagger under the weight of the debts owed their retired employees.

Moreover, part of American industry is threatened by the arrival of the Internet: everything that can be liquidated is progressively traded free of charge. The music industry already sells fewer CDs than ten years ago; attempts to replace CD sales by sales of digital files meet with failure. In 2005, out of the twenty billion digitized musical files fewer than one billion were purchased.

Salary-earners are also increasingly indebted, especially in regard to two public corporations (Fannie Mae, second-ranking American corporation, and the fifth-ranked Freddie Mac), which hold or stand behind five trillion dollars' worth of mortgage loans, a debt multiplied by four in ten years. Savings rates on American salaries are now only 0.2 percent, the world's lowest—whereas in the 1900s up until 1980 they stood at 7 percent. Between 2005 and 2008, Americans were spending virtually as much as they earned. Competition among lenders is tooth and nail. While bankers twenty years ago grumbled when 30 percent of a household's income was earmarked for repayment of these debts, in 2008 they consider a debt of 50 percent quite tolerable. In September 2008, the United States Treasury placed Fannie Mae and Freddie Mac under federal conservatorship.

Furthermore, disparities between the richest Americans and all the others soar. Between 1950 and 1970, for every dollar earned by 80 percent of the less fortunate members of the American population, the top one-tenth of one percent earned 162; today that imbalance stands at 1:250. In short, half of the wealth created from 1990 to 2008 has benefited 0.1 percent of households. The American worker's salary has been dropping since 1973 because of competition from immigrants and from relocation of businesses. In 2008, American salaried employees work an annual average of forty-six weeks, or six weeks more than Europeans, and they are allowed only half the annual vacation enjoyed by Europeans.

In 2008, even in California, where the minimum hourly wage is at least in principle eight dollars, one child in five lives below the poverty line. Between 2.3 and 3.5 million sedentary Americans are homeless every year. Almost one out of ten black children and one Hispanic child in twenty lives at least two months a year in a shelter. This is also true of one out of ten elderly people. In New York, more than thirty-eight thousand people are housed each night in municipal shelters, including sixteen thousand children. By 2008, some forty-seven million Americans, or 16 percent of the population, have no health insurance of any kind.

In the world at large, disparities become more and more extreme. Some 1.4 billion people live below the poverty line (estimated at $1.25 a day); by 2008, 1.3 billion people live on less than a dollar a day. The minimum hourly salary of a Californian is four times greater than the daily wage of a third of humanity. Half the world's population has no access to running water, education, health care, credit, or housing. Seventy-eight percent of the inhabitants of the villages of the southern hemisphere live in slums. Slum dwellers make up 99.4 percent of Ethiopians. Cities grow in disorderly fashion:

Dhaka, Kinshasa, and Lagos see their populations double from 1950 to 2008. There are some 200,000 shantytowns throughout the world. According to a June 2006 UN report, nearly one out of three people live in a shantytown. The planet's forty-nine poorest cities, accounting for 11 percent of the global population, still receive only 0.5 percent of world GDP.

World agriculture is stagnating, while populations grow increasingly swiftly and still suffer from hunger. To feed the world's population in 2050, world agricultural production will have to increase two and a quarter times! The number of available calories per head of population rises by only 3 percent between 1994 and 2008. In the latter year, 850 million people suffer from malnutrition — more than ever before. One billion people (a third of them women) are illiterate; more than 150 million children between six and eleven do not go to school.

Growth aggravates the destitution of many. A considerable proportion of the goods exported at very low price (clothing, toys, sports articles) to the shops of Europe and America is manufactured by ruthlessly exploited workers in the poorest countries of Asia and Latin America. One hundred fifty-eight million children aged four to fourteen — that's one out of six — are forced to work. Never in the course of history have so many people — estimated between twelve and twenty-seven million — been enslaved. In 2008, twenty-three thousand children die in work-related accidents. In Bangladesh, for example, the minimum monthly wage in the export business does not exceed ten dollars a month and, despite riots, has not been revalued since

1994. Children work seven days a week: salaries represent less than 10 percent of production costs. And nobody looks into anything.

In Africa the situation is even worse. Between 1987 and 2008, per capita revenue drops by a fourth. As a result, sub-Saharan Africa's debt has quadrupled, from $45 billion in 1980 to $175 billion in 2003, and the public foreign debt of Africa as a whole has gone from $89 billion in 1980 to $231 billion in 2004. In that same year, 2003, AIDS, a disease that appeared in the early eighties, afflicted over twenty-four million people, many of them adults under forty (teachers, young managers, policemen, soldiers), destroying the human infrastructure of these countries and leaving twelve million children orphaned. Only twenty-seven thousand receive treatment, since the cost of the highly active antiretroviral therapy (HAART) they need is twelve thousand times higher than what the average African annually spends on medication.

Where the status of women is particularly dire — from North Africa to northern India, whatever the prevalent religion — deprivation is even harsher.

Given these terrible disparities, population movements speed up. By 2008, especially in Africa, more than a fifth of the inhabitants live far from their birthplace. This is also the case with a fifth of Australia's inhabitants, a twelfth in the United States, and a twentieth of European Union residents.

Moreover, violence has never abated. While there is currently no declared war, the waning of East-West conflict has cast a pitiless light on the gap between North and South. Civil wars flare everywhere, from the Balkans to Latin America, from Africa to the Middle East.

No sooner has the Berlin Wall fallen in July 1991 than Iraq—one of America's new secular allies—believes it can profit from America's support to seize Kuwait's oil. After the Gulf War (in the course of which U.S. troops are stationed near Saudi Arabia's Holy Places), it has to abandon the effort. Shortly thereafter, Sunni and then Shiite pirates—used by the United States in the seventies to counter Soviet influence—turn against Washington. Attacks aimed at driving the "infidel" from holy ground and then from Arab lands multiply. In the first years of the third millennium of the Christian era, in Arabia, Africa, New York, then in Afghanistan, Iraq, and Lebanon, a part of Islam, once so deeply hostile to the Soviet Union, becomes the enemy of capitalism, of the United States and its allies. On September 11, 2001, pirates obsessed with theology turn to nomadic methods (civil aircraft) to destroy sedentary monuments (the New York towers).

Once again, the United States must now increase its security expenses to protect itself domestically and to attack abroad those it designates as responsible. It therefore declares an open-ended war in Afghanistan, and then in Iraq. Quagmire: the projected cost of the war in Iraq alone is estimated to cost over three trillion dollars, 2.5 percent of the American GDP. Once again, for the ninth time, the defense costs of a core threaten its survival.

In all, the mercantile order has thus far known nine successive forms around nine cities: Bruges, Venice,

Antwerp, Genoa, Amsterdam, London, Boston, New York, and finally Los Angeles.

The future, which seems to smile endlessly upon America, should nonetheless seek inspiration in the lessons of the past. It could in fact, for better or worse, resemble it: should the ninth form decline a tenth would appear, amid new geopolitical, economic, technological, and cultural upheavals, with a new core and new losers.

The history we have just outlined will help us trace that of the future and detect its dangers, so that hopefully we can master them.

3

The End of the American Empire

As we have seen, history viewed over the long term has hitherto obeyed a few simple rules. Since the emergence of democracy and the market, evolution is moving in one single direction. From generation to generation, it spreads individual freedom and channels desires toward their mercantile end. From century to century, farmers have migrated into cities. From century to century, the forces of market democracy have coalesced into an ever-growing and more integrated market around a temporary core. To assume power over the mercantile world — to become its core — a city or a region must be the biggest communication center of its day, and must be endowed with a very powerful agricultural and industrialized hinterland. This core must also be capable of creating banking institutions bold enough to finance the plans of an innovative class, putting new technologies to work, allowing the transformation of the most daunting services into industrial objects. And finally, the core must be able to exert political, social, cultural, and military control over hostile minorities, lines of communication, and sources of raw materials.

Today, everything seems to indicate that Los Angeles, the ninth core of the mercantile order, will be able to maintain that role for years or even decades.

But the current form of capitalism lives under the same threats as those that finished off previous forms. Its security is imperiled, its innovative class can no longer be trusted, industrially promising technical progress is slower and slower, and financial speculation is out of control. Disparities worsen, anger rumbles, and deep indebtedness piles up. Most disturbing of all is the flagging of the core's will to persevere at the top.

One day, in thirty years at the most, this ninth form (just like its predecessors) will bump against its limits. Once again, the market will work against the core: a new technology will replace other services with other industrial products. After the automobile, household equipment, and nomadic objects will come other major objects launched by a new core, ideologically, militarily, and culturally more dynamic, and centered around another project.

Before this happens, countless events will occur, most of them in history's direct line.

The Beautiful Future of the Ninth Form

Never has the Californian innovative class been so inventive, rich, and promising. Never have Californian living standards been so high. Never have the profits of the great American corporations reached such peaks. Never has the military and technological might of the United States been greater. Never have industrial and financial innovation been so triumphant. Never has the United States so clearly dominated the world — militarily, politically, economically, culturally, and even, to a certain extent, demographically: today it is the world's third most populous country, and with around 350 million inhabitants it will still hold that rank in 2040.

What is more, there is no credible rival on the horizon, either in Europe, Asia, or anywhere else. And it seems that no other model for development is even imaginable. Therefore (at least until 2025), the wealthiest people and most central banks will still consider the United States and the dollar as their best economic, political, and financial refuge. (Witness the recent strengthening of the U.S. dollar and the decline of the euro since the 2008 financial crisis began.) In particular, the American tax system (soon to do away with the essentials of the inheritance tax) will attract exotic fortunes even more powerfully than now. American universities will also be able to reconstitute the country's innovative class by recruiting some of the world's best students — who will then stay on to create.

Los Angeles will remain the country's cultural, technological, and industrial center, Washington its political capital, and New York its financial metropolis. The United States will long control defense technologies, data transmission, microelectronics, energy, telecommunications, aeronautics, motors, materials, guidance systems. It will maintain its role in world production for a long time. Its deficits will go on functioning as devices to spur consumption in the United States and production elsewhere. In all, during the next two decades at least (and even if U.S. growth might be temporarily interrupted by financial crises, recessions, or conflict), the essentials of cultural, political, military, aesthetic, moral, and social happenings will simply accentuate the primacy of the United States.

This primacy has been sustained by the 2008 election of President Barack Obama. He will have to face huge financial, economic, monetary, and social issues. Obama's leadership of America will also represent a serious shift from an emphasis on American hard power to a more cooperative power. This shift will occur through a slow decrease in military spending and stationing of troops overseas to a stronger emphasis on European-style diplomacy and welfare statism. Obama may represent, therefore, a first step in the transition from global superpower to the future cooperative status of the United States, more focused on domestic matters and ready to accept more multilaterism in the international arena.

For as long as it is able to defer other futures (and we will return to this), world growth will remain at its present average of roughly 4 percent per year. In 2030, if current trends (which give only a very vague notion of the future, even one twenty years from now) persist, world GDP will have grown 80 percent, and the average income of every inhabitant of the planet by a half. In 2060, China and India alone will account for roughly half the world's GDP. A significant section of the poorest will have entered the market economy as workers and as consumers. Products adapted to their purchasing power (food, clothing, housing, medicine, appliances, financial products) will be commercialized. Emigrants will finance their countries of origin by sending their savings home. Microcredit (which already gives access to financing for a working implement to more than 100 million entrepreneurs) will expand by 2025 to at least 500 million heads of families. Microinsurance will guarantee minimum social cover to the poorest of families. Even if half the world's population will still be surviving on only $1.25 a day by 2025, the share of world population participating in the market economy and knowing how to read and write will have increased considerably.

Along parallel lines, this economic growth will extend democracy's scope — no authoritarian government has ever resisted abundance for too long. The most recent of them (from General Franco to General Suharto, from General Pinochet to General Marcos) proved incapable of exploiting rapid growth in order to maintain their control over the middle classes. Most countries not yet market democracies (China, North Korea, Burma, Vietnam, Pakistan, even Iran) could join their ranks. Governments, institutions, administrations, police, and judiciary apparatus will heed elected parliaments, but they will no longer obey single parties or theological authorities.

During these two next decades, the European Union will probably be no more than a simple common economic space, enlarged to include the former Yugoslavia, Bulgaria, Moldova, and Ukraine. Even if its currency is likely to be used increasingly throughout the world, the union will most probably fail to build integrated political, social, and military institutions for itself. For this to happen, its security must be put under serious threat, which will not be appreciated until later, when the second wave of the future (which we shall soon examine) begins to break. In the absence of a modernized higher education system and the ability to kindle innovation and welcome foreigners, the union will continue to fail both at assembling a new innovative class and at luring back the researchers and entrepreneurs who have crossed the Atlantic. In the absence of an adequate demographic dynamic, the replacement of past generations will not be guaranteed, particularly in Spain, Portugal, Italy, Greece, and Germany. If current trends can be projected ahead, the union will account for only 13 percent of world GDP—as against 31 percent today. The per capita GDP of a European will be only half that of an American, compared with 70 percent today. This will also lead to lower-quality public services, from transport to education, from health to security. In a confrontation between Flanders and Wallonia, Brussels (after many ups and downs) could become a European federal district bereft of national ties. Naturally, a strong-state political upheaval could change this likelihood.

Eleven other economic and political powers will emerge—Japan, China, India, Russia, Indonesia, Korea, Australia, Canada, South Africa, Brazil, and Mexico. Later on I shall call them the *Eleven*. In twenty or twenty-five years, all of them will be market democracies or leaning heavily in that direction. Below them, twenty other fast-growth countries will still suffer from institutional weaknesses. These countries include Argentina, Iran, Vietnam, Malaysia, the Philippines, Venezuela, Kazakhstan, Turkey, Pakistan, the United Arab Emirates, Algeria, Morocco, Nigeria, and Egypt. Still other countries, more modest in size—such as Ireland, Norway, Dubai, Singapore, and Israel—will play a special role.

Asia will dominate. Two-thirds of the world's commercial exchanges will be transacted across the Pacific. In a little over twenty years, Asia's output will surpass half that of the rest of the world. Thirteen of the twenty biggest container ports (including Shanghai, Hong Kong, Singapore, Nagoya in Japan, Pusan in Korea, Kaohsiung in Taiwan, Dampier in Australia) are in Asia. Pusan (Pusan Newport) and Shanghai (Yangchan) are already capable of handling ninety containers per hour. Immense port and airfield infrastructures are still to be developed there.

In 2025, China (with almost a billion and a half inhabitants) will be the world's second-ranking economic power. At the present pace, its GDP will outstrip Japan's in 2015 and America's in 2040. Its share of world GDP, currently at 4.5 percent, will rise to 7 percent in 2015 and will be close to 15 percent in 2025. Its average standard of living should by 2050 rise to one-half that of Americans. Even if China's annual growth rate is half that of today, by 2025 it will have an annual per capita income of six thousand dollars. Hundreds of millions of Chinese will by then belong to the middle class, and several tens of millions to the upper classes. China will then have an excess in the balance of capital. It will continue to finance the U.S.'s deficits, just as if the two countries had a long-lasting pact aimed at maintaining world growth to their own benefit — until they reach the day when they feel strong enough to come to blows. From the Philippines to Cambodia, China will become the leading investor in the region, to the detriment of Japan and the United States If they are able to master their rural migrations, China's coastal regions will even become the meeting point of a innovative class from every corner of the globe, and in particular of returnees from the Chinese diaspora.

The Chinese Communist Party will be less and less able to organize urban life. It will be forced to leave power to elected officials in every city. Unless it reforms, it will fail to resolve its present immense difficulties: 90 percent of Chinese still have no retirement plan or health insurance; half the urban and four-fifths of the rural population have no access to medical care; half the country's five hundred biggest cities lack drinkable water or a sewage system. China will have to build an urban infrastructure, consolidate monetary stability, fight corruption, put a permanent stop to corruption in public finance, find work for hundreds of millions of peasants flowing into the cities, reduce the income gap, improve the education system, train many more managers, reform an obsolete public sector, and install a judicial system capable of protecting private and intellectual property—a wealth of tasks practically impossible under a single-party government. Around 2025 the Communist Party, by then in power for seventy-six years (no other party in the world has ever remained in power for more than seventy years), will in one way or another fade away. Great disorder will reign for a time, as has so often been the case in the country's history. A new democracy might even emerge, looking very much like the warlord-dominated democracy of 1912. If China then fails to maintain its unity (a possibility that cannot be discounted), it will participate in the general process of nation-deconstruction (we will return to this in the next chapter). In order to survive, the Chinese

Communist Party might also (as we will see) be tempted by a foreign adventure, such as invading Taiwan or Siberia.

India—with its 1.4 billion inhabitants—should be the most populous nation on earth by 2025 and the third-ranking economic power behind China and the United States. By 2010 its growth rate will surpass China's, but because of its superior population growth, its per capita GDP will remain lower than its neighbor's. Many of India's businesses, such as Tata, Infosys, or Mittal, will rank among the world's largest. For this scenario to happen, Indian democracy must surmount major challenges, very similar to those facing China. It must finance urban infrastructures, find alternative energy sources, construct highways and airports, launch a long-term cleansing of public finances, and reduce disparities among regions and social classes. If the central government fails to do so, the situation might lead, as in China, to a splintering of the country. Remember: India has been united only since the end of British colonial domination.

As for Japan, it will go on aging and declining in relative value, despite the economic strength that will continue to maintain its ranking as one of the very first global leaders. Unless it plays host to more than ten million foreigners or manages to boost a birth rate already in decline, its population will shrink. Although it is exceptionally well placed to dominate future technologies, from robots to nanotechnologies, Japan will not succeed in making individual freedom its predominant value. It will suffer increasingly from an encirclement complex—by North Korea's arms, South Korea's products, and China's investments. It will certainly react militarily by endowing itself with every kind of weapon (nuclear ones included) in an increasingly defensive and protectionist strategy. This could cost it very dearly on the economic front. By 2025 it is conceivable that it will no longer be the world's fifth-ranked economic power.

Among the other Eleven, South Korea will become one of Asia's leading powers. Its per capita GDP should double between the present and 2025: it will be the new economic and cultural model, and will impress the world with its technologies and cultural energy. The Korean model will be increasingly studied in China, Malaysia, the Philippines, and even Japan as the success story to emulate, rather than the American model. The life span of Korea's success story will depend on its ability to forge a pathway between two catastrophic scenarios: first, a reunification process brought about by the sudden collapse of the North Korean government; and second, military (and perhaps nuclear) escalation provoked by the inability of the North Korean regime to face its problems squarely—which would obliterate more than fifty years of the South's economic miracle.

By 2025, Vietnam will have more than 125 million inhabitants. If it succeeds in reforming its political, banking, and education systems, if it manages to build highway infrastructures and fight corruption, it will become Asia's third-ranking economy. In any event, it will certainly be a major actor and a magnet for foreign investors.

Indonesia will suffer from virtually insoluble problems: corruption, the weakness of its educational system, serious ethnic tensions among its hundred nationalities. If it manages to surmount them (which appears unlikely), it will become a great world economic power —and most assuredly in the Islamic world—for by 2025 it will have 280 million inhabitants. It possesses an abundance of natural wealth to help the process along (oil, gas, gold, silver, nickel, copper, bauxite). The likeliest outlook is that, as with China and India, growth will not be enough in the long term to calm the archipelago's separatist claims. Indonesia, like China, India, and so many others, may later break up into a score of smaller entities. We shall be returning to this.

Russia could rediscover a better demographic equilibrium and use a part of its oil income to foster its development. In 2008 it became the world's leading producer of black gold, outstripping Saudi Arabia (producing almost ten billion barrels per day, some 10–12 percent greater than Saudi Arabia), and its leading titanium producer. In 2025 its GDP should overtake those of Italy and France. Thanks to the cash reserves piled up from petroleum sales, it will have the means to purchase Western Europe's industry, which would cost it less than modernizing its own factories. Petroleum will continue to supply half its fiscal revenues. Like the other Eleven, it will have to put in place an urban infrastructure, a judicial framework protecting private and intellectual property, a modern banking system, and above all an improved health system. Russian life expectancy (which by 2008 had shrunk to fifty-nine years for men and seventy-two for women) will begin to rise again. In 2025 its population should stabilize at around 120 million, as against 142 million today. As we shall later see, Russia will also have to face new threats — Muslims from the south, Chinese from the east.

In Latin America, two powers will stand out in about 2025. With 125 million inhabitants, Mexico could achieve a GDP surpassing that of France. But the country will experience difficulties in avoiding unchecked growth in its cities, and in putting an end to very serious pollution and extreme disparities among its social classes and ethnic groups. Anti-American political revolts might hamper its growth and could even threaten its alliance with the United States. Brazil (with 229 million inhabitants by 2025) could then become the world's fourth-ranking economic power, behind the United States, China, and India, and ahead of Japan. Most important, it will become one of the giants of agriculture and agrobusiness. If we extend current trends (which, we should remember, give a very hazy idea even of the immediate future), its GDP will surpass Italy's by 2025, and then those of France, Great Britain, and Germany. To succeed in this, Brazil too will have to overcome challenges that today seem almost insoluble. It must install an urban infrastructure, build a solid and effective state, fight corruption, improve its education system, reform its obsolete public sector, and develop its export industry.

Unlike the other continents, Africa will probably fail to generate broad middle classes, although it may still experience very strong economic growth — largely balanced by even stronger population growth. In 2025 the continent will have more than 1.4 billion inhabitants. Nigeria, Congo, and Ethiopia will by then have joined the ranks of the world's most densely populated countries. Even though Africa's soil contains 80 percent of the world's platinum and 40 percent of its diamonds, even though Africa's forests overshadow unexploited resources and tourist wealth, even though China, India, and other countries (in search of the raw materials they need) go there to build low-cost infrastructures, the African continent will still fail to become an economic player of global importance. There are many reasons for this. The climate hampers the organization of labor; climatic upheavals (we will return to them) will lead to a 20 percent reduction of harvests in semiarid zones and the destruction of exploitable lands in humid regions, so that in 2025 Africa will be able to feed only 40 percent of its population. Its active population, decimated over the centuries by the slave trade and today by AIDS and other pandemics, will remain insufficiently trained. Once again, the elites will emigrate. Most African countries continue to be ravaged by political disorder, corruption, and acts of violence. Many "artificial" countries patched together during the colonial era, such as Nigeria and Congo, will teeter on the verge of explosion. In 2025, the continent will still have a per capita income below a quarter of the world average. Half of all Africans will go on struggling to survive with an income below the poverty threshold; the figures for malnourished children could climb as high as forty-one million. Only a handful of African countries will rise above this fate: South Africa (with a per capita GDP which will be higher than that of Russia), Egypt, Botswana, and perhaps Ghana. The other African countries will be threatened by blow-up—yet fragmented, they will be at risk of becoming nonstates.

And finally, the Arab world's share of world GDP will increase, but lethargically, with population increase counterbalancing that of productivity. In the absence of political stability, of a legislative framework, of separation of the religious and the secular, of implementation of the laws on men's and women's rights, the Arab per capita GDP will not rise as fast as that of the rest of the world—except in the northwestern Maghreb. There, the probable reconciliation of Algeria and Morocco will create the right conditions for a common market with the countries on the southwestern shores of the Mediterranean, and very promising cooperation with the countries of southern Europe. Next door, Turkey and Iran will be on the way to becoming major powers.

In all, this enduring world growth—the longest-lasting and the highest in the history of humanity—will go hand in hand with a tremendous acceleration in the implementation of globalization and the merchandising of time.

The Marketing of Time

People's time will be increasingly expended on commercial activities, which will replace services, whether gratis, voluntary, or forced. Agriculture will be increasingly industrialized; it will send hundreds of millions of workers toward the cities. World industry will be increasingly global, with borders ever more open to capital flows and goods. More and more easily, factories will migrate to wherever the overall cost of labor is lowest, in other words to East Asia and then India. The most sophisticated services and research centers, and the headquarters of the biggest corporations, will move into countries of the southern hemisphere where English is (and will remain) one of the national languages. In every local market, corporations will offer no more than the market studies necessary for the commercialization of their products as well as post-sale services.

Innovations will multiply with increasing swiftness. The cycle from creation to production and commercialization of food products and clothing will shrink from a month to four days; for automobiles and household products, already reduced from five to two years, it will soon be six months; for medicines it will fall from seven to four years. The life span of commercial brands will also be shorter and shorter; only the best ensconced and the best known globally will resist this lure of the new. The life span of buildings and houses will also be shorter. Shareholders in the big corporations will themselves be increasingly volatile, capricious, disloyal, and indifferent to the long-term needs of the businesses in which they invest, caring only for the immediate benefits they hope to receive in return. Bankers will insist that businesses reveal their accounts at ever closer intervals. Corporate leaders will be increasingly judged on short-term criteria, and will only keep their jobs for as long as they respond to a versatile market. Competition among workers, both in the workplace and in the search for work, will be increasingly harsh. Even more than today, knowledge (under permanent challenge from innovations) will be a major player. Early training will remain essential: everyone will have to retrain himself in order to stay employable. The long-term decline of birth rates and continued rise of life expectancy will lead to a shorter work year but a longer working life span. Retirement age will rise to seventy for all those whose work is neither arduous nor harmful to themselves or others. The oldest will serve as tutors, communicators, or consultants. The "wellness" industry will become a major enterprise.

It will become harder and harder to discern any difference between work, consumption, transport, entertainment, and training. Consumers will play an expanding part in conceiving products increasingly made to measure and available just in time. Consumers in the core and the "middle" will remain deeply indebted without—as Tocqueville thought long ago—feeling any more burdened by their debt than by a self-imposed limit on the consumption frenzy. Consumers will remain the masters and their interests will outweigh those of workers.

More than half of all workers will change their residence every five years, and they will change employers even more frequently. City dwellers in the northern hemisphere will finance their principal residence more and more through easily transferable mortgage credits.

More and more, city dwellers will live far from the centers: a household living within the city in 2008 will live eight miles from the center ten years later—and twenty-five miles farther out in 2025. New professions will surface to structure the logistics of this nomadic trend.

The ninth form will also go on creating the conditions for increasingly solitary urban living in smaller and smaller apartments, with increasingly fleeting sexual or romantic partners. Fear of being tied, flight from lasting attachments, and obvious indifference will become (are already becoming) forms of seduction. Apologia for the individual, the body, and independence.

Individualism will make absolute values of the ego, the self. Eroticism will become an openly sought field of knowledge. Apart from incest, pedophilia, and sodomy, the most diverse forms of sexuality will be increasingly tolerated. Nomadic ubiquity and virtual communities will create new opportunities for encounters, paid or not.

The secondary residence, inherited from previous generations, will become the principal habitat, the only fixed point for city dwellers. Tourism will evolve into a quest for silence and solitude; sites (religious or secular) for meditation, isolation, retreat, or inaction will proliferate. The sedentary lifestyle will be the last privilege enjoyed by children. They will often live with their grandparents while their parents—more and more likely to be separated—will take turns spending time with them.

Transportation will require increasing time; it will become a place for life, encounters, work, shopping, and entertainment. The time spent on commuting will be counted as working time, the way night and Sunday work have become universally accepted. Travel will turn into a major component of university and professional education; people will constantly have to demonstrate aptness for traveling in order to stay employable. Every European city with more than a million inhabitants will be connected through a continent-wide network of high-speed trains. More than two billion passengers, most of them business tourists, will fly every year; air taxis will enjoy massive patronage; at any moment, more than ten million people will be in the air. Pilotless city vehicles (much less costly than those now in use), made of lightweight materials, energy-efficient and biodegradable, will be the collective property of subscribers who will turn them over to others after each use.

New property legislation will emerge. It will give access (in every new place of residence) to housing of predetermined quality and size, and detached from a concrete site. In particular, the dematerialization of information will make it easier to move from ownership of data to its use, giving access to culture, education, and information. Verification of intellectual property rights will also be increasingly difficult to guarantee.

In every consumer sector, very low-cost products will be put in circulation. They will admit the poorest people of every country into the market economy, and will allow the middle classes to devote a shrinking part of their income to the purchase of food products, computers, cars, clothing, and household equipment.

The bulk of middle- and upper-class income will be used for the purchase of services such as education, health, and security. To finance them, the share of taxable income will increase, in the form of taxes and contributions. More and more people will opt for entrusting their risk coverage to private insurance companies, which — to the detriment of nation-states — are growing ever more powerful. Commercial, digital, and financial exchanges will increasingly take place beyond the reach of states — thus depriving them of a significant slice of their tax revenue. Public administration will be overturned by the use of new methods of communication (particularly of the Internet), which will permit the running of public services at lower cost and with immediate results.

To manage this merchandised time, two industries will dominate (as they already do): insurance and entertainment.

On the one hand (to shield him against risk), the rational response of every player on the market will be (and already is) to insure himself, in other words to protect himself against future uncertainties. Insurance companies (and the risk coverage institutions of the financial markets) will complete social security regimes and will become — if they are not already — the planet's leading industries, both for their turnover and the profits they reap. For the poorest, microinsurance will be an essential tool in reducing insecurity.

To escape financial insecurity, on the other hand, everyone will want to amuse himself — in other words to protect and to distance himself from the present. Entertainment industries (tourism, movies, television, music, sports, live shows, and shared play space) will become — unless they already are — the planet's leading industries, judging from the time it takes to consume their products and services. The media will enjoy a greater hold over democracy and over citizen choices.

Both options will also be the pretext for illegal activities: racketeering is the criminal face of insurance; drugs and the sex trade are the criminal versions of entertainment.

Every business and every nation will organize

themselves around these two needs—self-protection and distraction from fear of the world.

Nomadic Ubiquity

Before 2030 everyone but the poorest will everywhere be connected to every high-capacity information grid—both mobile (HSDPA, WiBrow, WiFi, WiMAX) and stationary (optical fiber). Everyone will thus be in a state of nomadic ubiquity. It has already begun: Google recently made available to the citizens of Mountain View (the California city where its headquarters are located) and to those of San Francisco free and universal access to wireless and high-performance Internet. In Korea, whole cities are now equipped with HSDPA mobile phone networks that perform ten times more efficiently than the 3G, as well as access to mobile, high-output Internet (WiBrow). These digital infrastructures will also help communities toward better management of urban security, of chaotic transport, and of disaster prevention.

This network connection of members of the innovative class, dispersed over several sites (and not obliged to meet in the same core), will favor communal long-distance creation of software, services, products, and productions. New languages will make it possible to write programs intelligible to the greater number, and to structure information to give simultaneous access to data and to its meaning.

To make it more convenient to connect with these jointly created nomadic objects (the work of many minds), they will become lighter and simpler: the mobile phone and the computer will fuse and be reduced to the size of a wristwatch, a ring, a pair of glasses, or a memory card, integrated into clothing better adapted to the demands of movement. A universal nomadic object will function as a phone, calendar, computer, music player, TV, checkbook, identity card, or a keychain. Very low-cost computers, using open technologies (such as Linux), will allow access to these networks at infinitesimal cost. Personalized research engines will evolve more and more alongside cooperative sites, sites offering free exchange of contents, counseling sites, and nomadic radio and television.

Television will become a made-to-measure, differentiated tool. We will watch major networks much more rarely; teenagers already spend three times less than their parents in front of a TV set, and they have already been subscribers to the Internet six times longer. We will watch TV principally on nomadic objects and for live shows. Increasingly specialized, personalized made-to-measure channels will appear.

Content owners (editors, musicians, filmmakers, writers, reporters, actors, data processors, designers, fashion designers) will be unable to maintain the patents on their properties indefinitely, nor will the coded systems aimed at preventing the free circulation of music files and films. Authors will then be remunerated by digital infrastructures, which will receive rental fees and advertising revenue in return.

Before 2030, most paper media, particularly the daily press, will become virtual. They will offer increasingly instantaneous, increasingly cooperative, and increasingly made-to-measure community services, modeled on America's MySpace, Korea's OhMyNews, or France's Agoravox. Counseled by professional journalists, citizens will bring a new perspective to news and entertainment — more subjective, more passionate, less discreet, often on little-known or neglected themes. Some of these citizen-reporters will acquire a degree of fame. Their incomes will vary according to the popularity of their offerings; some blog creators already earn more than three thousand dollars per month. We shall witness the ultra-personalization of content, depending on the needs and focus of interest of each individual: a blending of texts, audio files, and selected video. Distinctions among press, radio, TV, and "new media" will be less and less relevant. To survive, the media must accept this unavoidable march toward free, participatory, and ultrapersonalized media.

Books too will become accessible on low-cost screens as delicate as paper, e-paper, and e-ink — a new nomadic object in the shape of a scroll, at last giving commercial reality to electronic books. They will not replace books but will have other uses, for ephemeral, constantly updated works, and written specially for these new media, such as the Sony Reader and Kindle.

By 2030, new artworks will mingle all media and all means of distribution. It will no longer be possible to distinguish between what is owed to painting, to sculpture, to film, or to literature. Books will tell stories with three-dimensional images. Sculptures will dance with the spectators to new kinds of music. Games will more and more become ways of creating, imagining, informing, teaching, and surveillance, of raising self-esteem and the sense of community awareness. Movies past and future will be viewable in three dimensions, completed by sensorial simulators and virtual smells. It will also become possible to conduct a long-distance conversation with a three-dimensional interlocutor and to broadcast three-dimensional concerts, plays, sports events, lectures, and classes. Domestic robots (their arrival hailed so long ago) will become universal in daily life. They too will be constantly connected to high-output grids in nomadic ubiquity. They will function as domestic help, as aides for the handicapped or the aged, as workers, and as members of security forces. In particular, they will become "Watchers." In Korea, for example, the goal is to outfit, sometime between 2015 and 2020, every home with such robots, designed to perform domestic chores.

Again before 2030, nomadic ubiquity will invade all previously industrialized services: packaging of food products, clothing, vehicles, and household goods will also become "communicative." Sensors will be built into materials, motors, machines, fluids, bridges, buildings, and dams to keep permanent long-distance watch over them. Products, machines, and people will also be equipped with an identity tag on a radio frequency, which will enable businesses to raise the quality of their products and the productivity of their factories and distribution networks. Consumers will know everything about their product's origins, including its itinerary from raw material to date of sale. They will be informed as soon as a child's mobile phone goes through the school gate; they will be able to order the gates of a private residence to open from a distance, order household equipment to turn on, or order the purchase of a product whose lack the shopper's freezer will already have detected. The most recent vehicles will have built-in error detectors—and will evolve with experience. Everyone will study (from a distance) at some far-off university, or will be the motionless visitor to a museum or a patient in a hospital on another continent.

With each of us connected in space and time, nomadic ubiquity will reverse its course in about 2030 to become, as we shall see, a kind of hypersurveillance. This will turn into a major characteristic of the mercantile order's next form (see below).

The Aging of the World

All over the world, commercial growth will favor the prolonging of life. With an intensity that will vary depending on the country, we shall witness (we are already doing so) a lowering of the birth rate and a steady climb in life expectancy, and hence a general aging of the population.

If current trends continue, life expectancy in developed countries should by 2025—only a generation hence—increase for men by 3.7 years and for women roughly three years, and will then approach the century mark. Furthermore, with the growth of freedom—especially the freedom of women—birth rates will sink to the point where renewal of past generations will no longer be possible in many countries. In Korea, for example, the fertility rate, which was roughly 4.5 percent in the 1950s, dropped to under 1.5 percent in 2000. Birth rates will decline even in the Muslim countries, where they remain the highest (they still reach the figure of seven children per woman in some regions of the Middle East).

By 2025, more than ten million Americans will be over eighty-five; the number of those over sixty-five will rise from 12 percent today to a staggering 20 percent! That number will reach 25 percent in Japan and 20 percent in China. In France, it now stands at 33 percent, and that nation's figures for those over eighty-five will have doubled in the next ten years.

In some countries, aging will be so extreme that populations will actually shrink. Compared to 2002, Japan's population may well have declined by 14 percent by 2050; in Italy, this figure will be roughly 22 percent, and in places such as Bulgaria, Georgia, the Baltic countries, Russia, and the Ukraine, it could be as much as 30 to even 50 percent due to mass emigration and low fertility rates.

With fewer children to care for, women will escape more easily from male domination and discover their place in society. This will help Islam to evolve, just as the other monotheistic religions have evolved—and for the same reasons. Older people will be in the political majority. They will insist on priority for the present, on price stabilization, and on shifting the burden to coming generations. They will consume specific products (cosmetic, dietetic) and user-adapted services (hospitals, medically equipped homes, assistance personnel, retirement homes). All will consume more medication and more hospital care, leading to a massive rise in medical expenses—and therefore in insurance spending—around the world.

For the active population, the burden of financing retirement will be increasingly onerous: in today's Europe, each working member of the population already foots the bill for a quarter of all retirees. By 2050 he or she will be financing more than half.

To maintain the current ratio of active workers to retirees, we must accept an increase either in taxes, in the birth rate, or in immigration. Countries that refuse to admit foreigners will see a population collapse. Those that accept them will see their population change. In the bosom of the European Union, people coming from Africa and their descendants could represent 20 percent of the population by 2025. By then, 42 percent of Brussels's population could comprise the descendants of immigrants originally hailing from Islamic lands and Africa.

Such a shift will imply vast population movements, which the United States will doubtless be better prepared than others to face or to accept. Above all, it will imply extraordinary urban growth.

Tomorrow, the Cities

Migrations will be on a vaster scale within countries of the southern hemisphere, from countryside to cities, from rural to urban destitution. No political authority, even in a dictatorship like China's, will succeed in slowing these movements. Such mutations have a long history: whereas there were eighty-six cities in the world with more than a million inhabitants in 1950, by 2015 there will be 550.

Urban growth will be phenomenal everywhere: in 2008, half of the world's population lived in cities; twenty-six of which boasted populations of ten million. By 2025, the planet will accommodate thirty cities with more than ten million inhabitants, and four agglomerations with more than twenty million. Tokyo and Bombay will be host to more than *thirty* million. Nine of the world's twelve most populous cities will be in the southern hemisphere (the only exceptions being Tokyo, New York, and Los Angeles). From 2008 to 2025, Chinese cities will have to welcome the equivalent of all Western Europe's population. By 2035, thirty-six cities (located mainly in the southern hemisphere, they include São Paulo, Mexico City, Bombay, Shanghai, Rio de Janeiro, Calcutta, New Delhi, Seoul, Lagos, and Cairo) will number more than ten million inhabitants, and the urban population in the southern hemisphere will practically have doubled to hit the four billion mark. By 2050, a billion inhabitants will live in fifty Asian cities, each numbering more than twenty million people — and even, in certain cases, more than thirty million.

We will thus need to triple or quadruple urban infrastructures within thirty years — a goal that in most cases will prove practically unattainable. A handful of cities will succeed in becoming livable. New products — cheap cement, for example — and new techniques in construction and the microfinancing of housing will make it possible to transform certain shantytowns into very profitable markets for businesses able to look ahead.

Unless we imagine that such urban transformations are less gigantic than these linear projections indicate, and unless we hope that we are witnessing a retreat toward middle-rank towns, these great cities will essentially be no more than juxtapositions of flimsy houses without street maintenance, police, or hospitals, surrounding a few wealthy neighborhoods turned into bunkers and guarded by mercenaries. Mafias will control immense zones outside the law (this is already the case) in Rio, Lagos, Kinshasa, and Manila. Formerly rural people, with a few members of the privileged classes, will be the primary organizers of new social and political movements demanding very concrete changes in people's lives. It is on them, and no longer on the workers, that the great economic, cultural, political, and military upheavals of the future will depend. They will be the engines of history, and in particular of the second and third waves of the future that we shall soon examine.

To flee these horrors, over the next twenty years, many will move to other southern hemisphere countries in search of pleasanter climates, wider spaces, and cities either more secure or closer to the northern hemisphere.

Masses of Chinese will move into Siberia. Vladivostok is already in large measure a city economically, humanly, and culturally Chinese. Similarly, more than half the population of Khabarovsk, a Russian city on the banks of the Amur River, originally came there from the other side. While China's Heilongjiang province on the Siberian frontier boasts as many inhabitants as Argentina in a territory as small as Sweden's, 70 percent of Russia's territory is fast losing people and its extremely fertile agricultural lands are being abandoned. Chinese are very much in demand to repopulate them. In the Urals, the officials of Sverdlovsk have just invited Chinese peasants to cultivate 250,000 acres of abandoned land. This flow will increase with the increasing incidence of Russo-Chinese marriages; a considerable mass of Chinese will invade Russia little by little. By 2025, there will be fifteen million foreigners working in Russia, or 20 percent of Russia's working population. Slavs will begin to see a revival of the age-old threat of Mongol invasions.

At the same time—around 2020—other mass movements will flow from central to southern Africa or to northern Africa; from Indonesia to Malaysia, from Malaysia to Thailand; from Bangladesh to the Gulf States; from Iraq to Turkey; from Guatemala to Mexico.

For many immigrants, these moves will simply be a way of approaching the countries of the North. Ever more numerous masses will hurl themselves at the gates of the West. They already number hundreds of thousands every month; that figure will increase to millions, then tens of millions. And not only from the most disadvantaged: all the elites of the South will leave for the North. Their major points of passage will be the Russian-Polish, Iberian-Moroccan, Turkish-Greek, Turkish-Bulgarian, Italian-Libyan, and Mexican-American borders.

The United States will continue to be the country most sought after by emigrants. In 2008, 1.6 million foreigners settled there. Only 600,000 did so legally. Twelve million people, or a third of all immigrants in America, entered illegally. Half of them come from Mexico, and a third from Central America. A growing number of people will try their luck in a lottery that decides the allocation of 50,000 American visas (there are already eight million candidates, 1.5 million of them from the Middle East). In twenty years, the Hispanic and African-American populations will almost constitute a majority in the United States. Their elites and those from Asia will reinforce American power. If present tendencies continue, the American population will rise from 281 million in 2000 to 357 million in 2025, and this demographic inflow will by itself explain the continuation of growth in the core of the ninth form.

After being lands of emigration, the countries of southern Europe will also become host countries. They will recover dynamism, growth, and the means to finance their retirements. Other European countries, such as France, will attempt to refuse these immigrants from Eastern Europe and from Africa, but will realize that a population inflow, well controlled and integrated, is the condition of their own survival. Great Britain will also become a major host country, especially for citizens of Central European countries. The latter will in their turn welcome Ukrainian workers, themselves replaced by Russians, themselves replaced by vast Chinese populations. In all, the inflow of immigrant workers into developed countries will make it easier to finance retirements but will weigh heavily on the salaries of the middle classes.

Moreover, more and more people will leave one country of the North for another: there will soon be more than ten million of them switching countries every year. Some of them will do it for professional reasons and will amply reinforce, as in the past, their lands of origin, for which they will continue to serve as economic, financial, industrial, and cultural ambassadors. Others, more and more numerous, will choose to leave simply because they no longer want to depend on a country whose tax system, legislation, and even culture they reject. And also to disappear completely, to live another life. The world will thus be increasingly filled with people who have become anonymous of their own free will; it will be like a carnival where everyone — ultimate freedom! — will have chosen a new identity for himself.

Finally, tens of millions of retirees will go to live — whether part-time or for good — in countries with kinder climates and a lower cost of living, particularly North Africa. Whole cities will be built for these newcomers, attracting hospitals, doctors, architects, and lawyers, who will make the move with their clients. This will last as long as native populations accept these new residents.

In all, twenty-five years from now, about fifty million people will exile themselves each year. Nearly one billion people will live elsewhere than in their native countries or in their parents' native countries.

Irretrievable Scarcities

Until now, the mercantile order has always managed — just in time — to come up with what is needed to replace raw materials growing scarce, sometimes at the price of military operations and the displacement of the core.

This is how the world successively overcame the disappearance of farmlands in Flanders, of charcoal in England, of whale oil in the Atlantic, of coal throughout Europe. The invasion of cities by horse droppings, feared by everyone in the late nineteenth century, never materialized. For the last century, the environment has even been considerably improved in countries of the core and the "middle." London's air, unbreathable in the nineteenth century, is much purer today, like that of all the industrial centers of the wealthy countries. Similarly, lack of energy (regularly foretold for over a century) is a fear that is daily receding. Yet since the start of the eighteenth century, consumption of raw materials has multiplied by thirty. Over just the past forty years, consumption of mineral resources has tripled, and since we began using petroleum 900 billion barrels have been burned.

Before 2035, the virtual doubling of urban populations will be accompanied by a doubling of the demand for raw materials. While it is certain that one day every one of them will become rare, and that on several occasions there will be a temporary lack of certain resources, they will all be available at the end of the twenty-first century; and the most precious of them, silver and gold, will still be available for at least two centuries. Moreover, we are beginning a massive recycling of industrial waste, thus recovering an important share of raw materials: 40 percent of aluminum production comes from recycled waste. And finally, when we really confront scarcity, we will hunt for iron, titanium, and other minerals in the oceans or on the moon.

For energy, however, the data are even more disquieting. At current rates of consumption growth, reserves stand at only 230 years for coal, sixty-four for gas, forty years for confirmed petroleum. But we must also take into account Venezuela's heavy petroleum and

Canada's bituminous sands. Those bituminous shales alone could represent as much energy potential as all of Saudi Arabia's petroleum, even though their extraction would be an ecological disaster calling for heavy use of energy. Extraction of petroleum from bituminous strata will again call for heavy spending (in the form of coal) and quantities of energy higher than the quantities recovered in the form of petroleum.

As for gas, it seems more durably abundant, even if it will require heavy investment in transport accompanied by major geopolitical risks. Besides, in twenty years it will be possible to convert coal economically into petroleum products, which will again double the quantity of petroleum available. For another century, the availability of oil will thus be only a question of price.

The progressive transition to other energy sources will therefore be essential. Where management of radioactive wastes is politically accepted, nuclear energy will be used more and more. There will be progress on issues such as safety, acceptability, and competitiveness, and in thirty years this energy will supply 15 percent of the world's primary energy needs. Solar and wind power will not be inexhaustible sources until the energy they produce can be stored. Biomass will be hard to develop on a grand scale except (which is very important) for powering private cars. The other sources of natural energy—geothermal, ocean swell, tidal—appear unable to respond to significant demand. Finally, thermonuclear fusion, which could on its own represent an almost inexhaustible source, will certainly not be practicable before the end of the twenty-first century at best. Overall, energy will be more and more costly, which will encourage consumers to economize by replacing physical movement with telecommunications.

Long before lack of energy really makes itself felt, other scarcities will have to be overcome, especially in farm and forest products. While we must double agricultural production before 2050 to feed the world's population (which implies one billion more tons of cereals per year, or 50 percent more than in 2008), almost fifteen million acres disappear each year under the pressure of urban development. What is more, humanity has already consumed half the capacity of plants to photosynthesize sunlight. Adequate agricultural development will therefore imply the use of genetically modified organisms (GMOs), whose harmlessness nothing and no one has so far guaranteed. And time is short: stocks are running out.

Forests will be rarer and rarer, devoured by the packaging and paper-making industries and by the expansion of agriculture and cities. The creation of farmland, which is more profitable than forest land, will also lead to mass deforestation. Since the eighteenth century, a part of the world equivalent to the whole surface of Europe has been stripped of its forests. In the last ten years of the twentieth century, half the forest reserves of the western region of Germany disappeared. The equivalent of five football fields is deforested every hour. Japan, the world's leading importer of timber, is responsible for a third of this carnage. Furthermore, industrial gases, sulfur, and nitrogen oxides randomly destroy trees across the globe, in particular the fragile shade-loving trees of the "periphery." And finally, development of the immaterial economy will take a long time to reduce the demand for printing paper. At the present pace, there will be no more forests in twenty years except in countries where they are nurtured—that is (for the time being), only Europe and North America. This disappearance will be lethal to countless living species, even threatening the survival of humankind.

Greenhouse gases released into the atmosphere by industrial production constitutes another threat. While production of fluorocarbons, which reduce the depth of the ozone layer surrounding the earth, now seems to be under control, twenty-thee million tons of carbon (produced by the combustion of carbon, petroleum, and gas) are annually released into the air—where they heat it. And other diverse gas emissions join in. It will get worse: China, whose carbon emissions in 2006 already exceeded those of the United States by almost 10 percent, plans to build the equivalent of a thousand-megawatt electric power station every month over the next thirty years, thus feeding greater and greater amounts of pollutants into the atmosphere. Unless we can imagine a colossal joint action between now and 2030, carbon gas emissions per capita will double.

The publication of the Global Carbon Project (GCP) in 2008 concerning the worldwide emission of carbon dioxide for the preceding year (2007) revealed that eight and a half billion tons of carbon were emitted from all sources, including the consequences of deforestation.

If the absolute value of these emissions is disturbing, the speed with which they are taking place is even more so. Since 2000, they have increased by an average of 3.5 percent per year, four times faster than in the decade from 1990 to 2000, when the annual increase was just under 1 percent. Why? Because while the industrial countries have for all intents and purposes not diminished their emissions, the developing countries, especially China and India, have increased theirs far more than expected.

This is where the worst danger lies, for according to most experts the carbon gas thus emitted will lead to a considerable rise in the atmosphere's temperature. While the average temperature of the earth's surface has increased by only three-quarters of a degree in the last hundred years, the last decade has been the hottest in history. And doubtless this phenomenon is only beginning. Despite the extreme variability of climates, the most reliable simulations predict that the earth will warm by three degrees before 2050 and by 6.4 degrees before 2100. The consequences are already there to be seen. The polar caps have begun to melt, at least in the North. The thawing speed of ice has risen by 250 percent from 2004 to 2008; the glaciers of Greenland, the second-leading source of freshwater, are rapidly shrinking. From 1990 to 2008, three million cubic kilometers of ice (out of the eight million that existed at the North Pole) have vanished; ocean levels are rising by two and a half millimeters per year and in 2050 will have risen by at least nineteen centimeters, perhaps even by fifty, and by some accounts by fifty-eight. The last time it has been so hot was in the middle of the Pliocene, three million years ago, when the ocean level stood at twenty-five meters higher than today.

Natural disasters will follow, with gigantic financial

consequences. With the marked increase in temperature changes, very important alterations will take place in nature. Trees will grow faster and will be more fragile; there will be more oaks and fewer beeches; cicadas will be at home in Scandinavia, along with the praying mantis and Mediterranean butterflies. Plankton will migrate northward, followed by the fish that feed on them, causing the disappearance of the seabirds for which they were the staple diet. Much more serious: many more coastlines could become uninhabitable. Seven of the world's biggest cities are ports, and a third of the world's population lives on a coastline. Each year, the African desert expands across a surface equal to the area of Belgium. Soon two billion people will be living in regions threatened by desertification, 700 million of them in Africa. Fifteen million have already had to leave their villages, now uninhabitable. According to the Office of the United Nations High Commissioner for Refugees (UNHCR), these eco-exiles will be ten times more numerous by 2050.

Emission of carbon gas and other polluting gases will not be easily reduced. The countries of the North will find it hard to modify their way of living, while those of the South will long reject all kinds of restrictions, arguing that they would merely be safeguarding the wealth and comfort of the North. Brazil will continue to burn the Amazonian forest for so long as the industrialized countries do not substantially reduce their own carbon gas emissions. The only international agreement on this issue, signed at Kyoto in 1999, will have practically no effect on these developments. Change will not be felt until the day the countries of the North perceive the extreme seriousness of the consequences, and when those of the South understand that investment from the North will be substantially reduced if they do not make the effort to reduce their energy consumption. This will begin, as we shall see in the following chapter, with a very decisive action by the market, under pressure from the insurance companies and from public opinion.

Drought will have another consequence — making drinking water ever scarcer. Here the facts are overwhelming: half of the world's rivers are already at risk of becoming seriously contaminated by industrial, agricultural, and urban pollution. The human race has already consumed 80 percent of its natural freshwater resources. There remain only eight thousand cubic meters of drinkable water per person per year, against nine thousand in 1990 and fifteen thousand in 1900. More than 2.5 billion people have difficulty gaining access to drinking water, and 3.5 billion to safe water. More than 200 million people annually contract cholera after drinking contaminated water. Polluted water kills twenty-two thousand people a day. It brings in its wake hundreds of diseases. Already very disquieting, this situation can only grow worse: by 2025, half the world's population will suffer a lack of drinking water, particularly in Africa, the Middle East, and South Asia. Between now and 2040, the amount of drinking water available per inhabitant will again sink by a half, falling to four thousand cubic meters per day. The case of Gaza is a good example: its well water has been so heavily exploited that the phreatic layer has been covered by the sea — itself polluted by the wastewaters released into it — because 40 percent of the inhabitants possess no flush or sewerage system. Any long-term solution, in Gaza as elsewhere, must begin with a better urban maintenance program, desalinization of seawater, and better management of the available drinking water. In fact, there would be freshwater in amounts sufficient for twenty billion people if we could better handle the quantities absorbed by agriculture and industry, double the seventy billion dollars annually expended on production, distribution, and management of freshwater, begin a large-scale program for desalinizing seawater — three times more available than freshwater — and impose a massive price rise for consumers or taxpayers.

Finally, animal and vegetable diversity seems to be dwindling as a result of the combined forces working to harm it. About sixteen thousand species disappear every year, out of the 1.74 million species already recorded and the fourteen million believed to exist. One-quarter of all mammal species are threatened with extinction; a tenth of the coral reefs (without which no life on land would have been possible) are already condemned beyond repair; another third are menaced with extinction between now and 2035. The manta ray, for example, is on the road to extinction, like four of the seven marine turtle species; the world population of hippopotamuses has shrunk by half in the course of the past five years; 80 percent of certain shark species have disappeared in the last ten years; cod might vanish entirely before the end of the century; bluefin tuna is becoming rare. In all, the number of animal species could fall by 90 percent, as it has done twice in the history of the globe (first 250 million years ago, then sixty million, when the dinosaurs vanished and mammals emerged). The disappearance of half of all living species before the end of the twenty-first century is not to be discounted. And it is by no means certain that the human species will survive.

As in the past, new technologies could emerge to overcome each of these forms of scarcity. Among other things, they should help to reduce energy consumption, to find better ways of ridding ourselves of wastes, and to rethink cities and transportation.

Stagnating Technology

Two technological advances have so far guaranteed the expansion of the new form, one of them permitting continuous increase in the storage capacity of information through microprocessors, and the other the storage of energy by batteries. By 2030, these two advances will have reached their limits. Moore's law (doubling microprocessor capacities every eighteen months) will have reached the end of the road, and around the same time the absolute limit of storage capacity for lithium batteries will be attained.

In other fields, linear innovations also seem to be slowing down. The automobile industry is stagnating, as is the home equipment industry. The cell phone and the Internet have made scarcely any progress for fifteen years; genetics is marking time; new drugs have not made their appearance; agriculture has made very little progress; new forms of energy have still to appear. Elsewhere, much false progress is heralded; personal computers are unnecessarily powerful, and cars too complex. In 2006 a laptop was ten times more powerful and ten times more expensive than those that could satisfy consumer needs today.

To meet our needs in energy, water, food, and clothing products, means of transport and communication, and to eliminate the wastes of a rapidly growing population, we must therefore solve scientific problems today beyond resolution by perfecting industrially effective logistical systems that are financially practicable and socially acceptable.

First of all, major progress should be made in the miniaturization of a great many processes, no longer by packing more and more energy into ever-shrinking spaces but by utilizing the infinitely small, living or not, as a machine. In particular, we must succeed in modifying sowing seasons to make agriculture less thirsty for water, fertilizers, and energy, and organize the storage of gaseous hydrogen in order to manufacture—in economically reasonable conditions—hydrogen under high pressure, and then hybrid motors continually producing hydrogen under high pressure via electrolysis. This is the goal of future technologies, both biotechnologies and nanotechnologies. But their validity, their practicability, their safety, and their political and social acceptability will not really be achieved until 2025 at the earliest.

What is more, to comply with the injunctions of the financial markets, the research laboratories of private enterprises will circulate their results more rarely and will take fewer and fewer risks. More generally, industrial businesses will be increasingly reluctant to take risks and invest in industry, preferring the benefits of financial speculation to those—more hazardous—of technique.

And finally, one scarcity seems very difficult to overcome: time.

Time: The Only True Scarcity

Production of commercial articles will take less and less time; and we shall also spend less and less of it cooking, cleaning house, eating. But products placed on the market will themselves be devourers of time. What will first of all increase is time spent on transportation, implicit in the growth rate of the cities. It will become a kind of stolen time, where people will go on eating and working. Moreover, more and more time will be spent in the course of transportation on communicating, gathering information, watching films, playing cards, watching shows. It will likewise be possible, while working, to listen to music or a taped book or to watch a live show. Music will increasingly become the great comforter in the face of sorrow, periods of mourning, solitude, and loss of hope.*

Despite this reduced time, many will realize that they will never have the time to read everything, hear everything, see everything, visit everything, or learn everything. Since available knowledge already doubles every seven years, and by 2030 will double every seventy-two days, the time needed to keep oneself informed, to learn, to become and remain employable will increase accordingly. It will be the same for the time

*Recent studies of the brain's reaction to music show that the effect on listeners is entirely positive, soothing, comforting, diminishing stress.

needed to take care of one's health and to entertain oneself. Whereas the time needed for sleeping or making love will remain unchanged.

To skirt this obstacle, which eats into consumption, the mercantile order first encourages storage of time-devouring objects — books, disks, films — in material fashion, then (today) in virtual form: unlimited stacks, illusory, no longer possessing any relation to the possibility of being used. As though this stacking served to give everyone the illusion that he will not die before reading all these books, hearing all these melodies, and living all this stored time. In vain. Besides, future works of art will center more and more around this now obsessive theme of time.

By now it will have become clear that time is in fact the only true scarcity: no one can manufacture it; no one can sell the time available to him; no one knows how to accumulate it.

There will of course be attempts to produce a little time by prolonging the human life span. The target will be an average 120 years, for a work week of twenty-five hours.

To go ahead a little further, it will be necessary to overthrow barriers (by definition immovable) by reducing the time spent fulfilling functions inherent in every life: being born, sleeping, learning, taking care of one's health, loving, deciding. For example, we must be able to bring a child to birth in less than nine months, teach him to walk in less than a year, and speak a language in less than three thousand hours.

Some will then find that freedom itself — humanity's major target since the beginnings of the mercantile order—is in fact only the illusory manifestation of a caprice within time's prison.

The Fate of the Ninth Form

Now the great crisis of this form is at hand. In fact, it is already well under way.This first financial crisis of the age of globalization can largely be explained by the inability of American society to provide decent salaries to its middle class; this is what forced them to go into debt to purchase their homes, which caused an artificial increase in the value of capital and the economy. The financial institutions and the "initiated" who lead them had set aside the principal wealth generated therein for themselves without running the least bit of risk, thanks to securitization (collateralized debt obligation) and insurance (credit default swap). This led to an increase in debt which soon enough became intolerable and created panic, bankruptcy, and a lack of trust. The situation at hand could very well lead to a global depression or, on the contrary, constitute the beginnings of tremendous harmonized growth. But growth assumes the systematic reduction of debts and not, as has been seen in the past, its transfer solely to taxpayers. This requires above all the re-enabling on a worldwide scale of the power of the markets by that of democracy. And first the re-empowerment of the financial markets by that of law; the empowerment of the initiated by that of the citizens.

From now until 2030, the ninth form, like all of its predecessors, will deal with the worldwide problems outlined above, as well as the challenges specific to any core, which will become increasingly expensive. But they will lead inevitably to the decline of the ninth form.

First of all, the economic crisis that surfaced in 2007 with the subprime and so-called toxic mortgages will result in the virtual liquidation of investment banks worldwide, to the disappearance of many hedge funds, and a widening problem for credit card companies. All of this will result in a massive rethinking, starting in 2009, of governments' role in finance and banking, of a substantial increase in taxes both corporate and personal, and the implementation of some sort of close international regulation of global financial systems, with Wall Street no longer the principal player. At the same time, while other currencies will challenge the dollar as the world's major reserve, the American currency will continue to dominate for decades to come.

Several other results will come of this phenomenon. The income of Americans, which has stagnated if not actually declined in recent years, will erode further, mainly because of two factors: first, the increasing competition of foreign workers, and second, the outsourcing of jobs. What is more, the combination of all the above, plus the realization of how great the difference is between the earning power of the average American and that of the wealthy — the top 1 percent — will raise the disturbing question: is the American dream still attainable?

The disaster in 2005 of Hurricane Katrina, and the revelation in the following years of the fragility of the country's public service — 30 percent of American bridges, it was found, are in need of serious repair — raised the question of whether the country is any longer capable of coping with its own internal problems.

Furthermore, over the past two or three decades, an ever greater portion of Americans' incomes will of necessity have to go toward paying for energy, water, education, security, retirement, and protection of the environment.

All this said, of the deep recession that I predicted would surface near the end of the first decade of the present century, the American economy, which has always been resilient, will rebound, led by the realms of insurance, health, technology, energy, and infrastructure. Since we have predicted that over the next several decades the cities of the world will double and triple in size, more and more of Americans' money will have to be spent on urban schools, hospitals, road repair—in fact all kinds of local needs the federal government cannot, or will not, pay for. As early as 2011, the United States will be a much changed society, a technological state democratic and international, but still the leader of the world. Where does this leave the ninth core twenty years from now?

My prediction is that at least until 2030 it will succeed in keeping its agriculture going, protecting its cutting-edge industries, perfecting new technologies, increasing the productivity of its services, modernizing its weapons systems, defending its commercial zones, guaranteeing its access to raw materials, and maintaining its strategic influence. Thus, California will remain the core, and the United States will keep its technological lead through massive public investments aimed at its strategic businesses, particularly in the military field, financed by a budget whose now yawning deficit will remain covered by international borrowing. Washington will remain on good terms with Europe and with the Eleven, so that these groupings will go on underwriting its borrowings and sharing the costs of its defense. In particular, the United States will do nothing to demand a massive reevaluation of the currency of these countries (and most especially the Chinese currency), which would nevertheless greatly facilitate the maintenance of jobs on American soil. Some of the Eleven and the Europeans will accept this alliance, which will allow them to maintain their growth without having to devote excessive sums to their own defense.

This program for the next twenty years is already in place. But year by year, from now to 2030, and just like the preceding cores, the ninth will have to confront the global difficulties we have already mentioned, and the increasingly costly challenges, inherent in every core, that will culminate in its decline and replacement.

Starting in 2015, a new challenge will come from virtual enterprises. If the Internet is now essentially an American colony, where English is spoken and where the bulk of its wealth is drained toward the mother country, this eighth continent will one day attain its autonomy. It will become a power in itself, an autonomous entity reaping profits outside America's borders. New powers in finance, information, entertainment, and training will play against American political and cultural power. They will give birth to a new diversity that will challenge America's financial, economic, political, ideological, and aesthetic domination of market democracy. It will become increasingly clear that one can be a democrat and favorable to the market economy, without necessarily speaking English and without believing in the natural and everlasting supremacy of the American empire.

Next, America's real enterprises will detach themselves from America. Facing increasing competition in numerous sectors from enterprises and research centers located elsewhere, U.S. strategic industries will exile their production and their research. As with the preceding cores, these firms will realize that their commercial interests are no longer in step with those of their government, whose increasingly degraded image will hamper sales of their products. First they will try first to elicit from the White House an attitude more in line with what their worldwide consumers need. Then (disappointed) they will distance themselves from the administration, invest less in American universities and hospitals, and create fewer jobs at home. Some of them will even accept control by foreign investment funds of indeterminate nationality. These funds will accumulate their profits in tax havens, thus depriving American shareholders of the bulk of the profits and denying the American state much of its tax receipts. The financial system — more and more concentrated around insurance institutions and funds for high-risk coverage that demand an increasingly elevated profitability — will find itself under threat.

All over America, the commercial frustrations of salaried employees will make themselves increasingly felt. The middle class, leading player in the market democracy, will rediscover the insecurity it believed it had escaped by dissociating itself from the working class. Downgraded managers, mistreated employees, families left abandoned, indebted owners, disappointed consumers, users in revolt, frustrated minorities, and religious believers will cry out against the impenetrability of their solitude, the enormity of the injustices around them, the violence of inequalities, the breakdown of communities. Concentration of populations in cities will create growing needs for urban maintenance, schools, hospitals, and all collective services — more and more difficult to finance by taxation, and whose inadequacy will trigger unrest among the minorities. In fact, the Katrina disaster of 2005 has already revealed the structural inequality of American public services and laid bare America's incapacity to handle its own infrastructure problems.

Expenditure on energy, water, health, education, security, retirement, and environmental protection will take up a growing share of everyone's earnings. Financing internal and external deficits will be increasingly arduous. The dollar will become a device more political than economic, thus putting a brake on its use by others, particularly in Latin America and the Middle East — where its use is nonetheless essential to U.S. power. The profitability of capital will be maintained only artificially, through the continued increase in the value of assets.

Elsewhere, in Latin America, Europe, Africa, Asia, and the Middle East, the Californian model will be under increasing challenge by about 2025, and the notion of American domination will be spurned. The model of market democracy will itself be contested, in the very arena of its success: small totalitarian states will succeed perfectly well, and market democracy will no longer be the only synonym for economic success or technical efficiency.

Thus, by around 2025 or 2030, the costs of America's internal and external organization will have increased to such a degree that the structural deficit of its balance of payments will become insurmountable. Asia, which will continue to guarantee the essentials of its financing, will now increasingly need its own resources to reduce inequalities among its own regions, struggle against urban unrest, and put in place its own system of social insurance and retirements. Beijing, whose political power will be threatened by the previous economic downturn, and will therefore take a tougher stand, will decide against further low-cost financing of the American deficit, and will even opt for repatriating its capital invested in American bonds. Other foreign central banks will also begin to balance their reserves in other currencies. The U.S. Treasury will have to propose a much higher return on its borrowings, thus raising the cost of new credit card contracts, mortgage loans, and debts indexed—like credit cards—at variable rates. American households will have to sell the housing they had offered in guarantee of their loans; the price of real estate in the United States will plummet; the credit pyramid, based on the value of American housing, will collapse. Indebted households will become insolvent. Insurance companies will insist on the payment of premiums. The federal government—itself now paralyzed, like the whole American financial system—will be unable to rescue the weakest. Production will slow and joblessness will reach hitherto unknown heights. The crisis could also come more directly from the inability of the financial system to hold on to its own savings, which will be invested in increasingly speculative fashion in funds managed on the Internet from tax havens. The profitability of capital will no longer be maintained by the rise in the value of assets. The financial crisis is about to explode.*

All this resembles what happened in times past to Venice, Genoa, Bruges, Antwerp, Amsterdam, London, Boston, and New York.

By around 2030, then, California will cease to attract the lion's share of the world's innovators and entrepreneurs or to be the center for implementation and financing of major industrial innovations. The ninth form will have lived its day.

The United States could then become a Scandinavian-style social democracy, or a dictatorship — and even perhaps one after the other. It would not be the first time such a surprise occurred: the first leader to apply the principles required to emerge from the crisis of the eighth form was Mussolini; the second was Hitler. Roosevelt came only third.

Along one route or another, a tenth form of the mercantile order could then see the light of day.

Is a Tenth Mercantile Form Possible?

During each of the nine previous transformations of the mercantile order, convulsions, lulls, and active resistance gave contemporaries the feeling that the form then in

*Has exploded. These words, prophetically, were written five years before the worldwide financial crisis occurred.

place, no matter how threatened, could never disappear, and that the core of the day would forever remain the capital of the world.

Often, in fact, power has long since changed hands without anyone, in the core or around it, truly realizing what had happened. The former masters continued to believe that they dominated the world with their products and their culture, through their diplomacy and their armies — whereas they had in fact entered an irreversible decline, and others had taken their place. So it was with the previous eight. So it will be tomorrow in California.

Yet if history has a direction, when this ninth form of the mercantile order fades away in thirty years or less, exhausted by the efforts required to combat its enemies, it will give place to another form, with another core, other technologies, other geopolitical relationships between the continents.

This is where the detailed account of history set out in the preceding chapters finds its justification — for it allows us to draw the future's face with precision.

If in fact this tenth form resembles its nine predecessors, it will strike new balances among nations. It will extend freedom of lifestyles. New technologies will permit a further reduction of the time needed to manufacture food, clothing, means of transport, and entertainment; new services will be transformed into industrial products; new workers into insecure salaried employees. New energy sources will replace those grown scarce; more and more wealth will be concentrated in the hands of a shrinking tally of the privileged; a much wider variety of choices will be offered to the consumer and the citizen, imposing new forms of alienation on the workers.

The core of this tenth form will have to be — once again — a vast region focused on a great port (or airport) in control of the world's commercial networks. In this new core, a particularly liberal and dynamic social climate should allow an innovative class to perfect (for its own benefit) ideas, techniques, and values capable of solving the challenges that will then face the mercantile order — in other words to reduce this time the costs of health, education, and security — and to introduce the new consumer products essential to the revival of global growth.

The likeliest scenario is that this tenth core will be situated for the fourth time somewhere in the territory of the United States. Even after the financial crisis of the first two decades of the twenty-first century, America will remain the leading military, technological, financial, and cultural power in the world. Without any conceivable competition, it will be the most immense market and the surest refuge for elites and capital. Washington will continue to be the political capital of the world, and the U.S. Army will still be the planet's leading military force — by far. And finally, America will one day restore its finances by finding the means — as it did with the automobile, then with household equipment, and then with nomadic objects — of reviving growth through industrial production (which we shall define) of new objects.

So that if a new American city were to become the tenth core, it would doubtless once again be situated in the neighborhood of California, which will in fact remain (for at least fifty years) the planet's most dynamic state, situated on the shores of the busiest ocean in the world. No other American state will be in a position to challenge it: New York State will be too weakened industrially. Texas, too isolated, will fail through lack of infrastructure.

This second Californian core (just as there were two successive cores on the East Coast, Boston and New York) would probably be located farther south, at the Mexican border. It would be at once in the neighborhood of another great country and of one of the Pacific's most dynamic ports (San Diego). It would be in the heartland of America's defense, space, telecommunications, and microelectronic industries, and of the most important centers for biotechnologies and nanotechnologies (La Jolla). Exceptionally brilliant students from all over the planet would continue to flock here to study in some of the world's best universities (Stanford and Berkeley). This tenth core, manufacturing new industrial products in response to future needs, would extend from north of Mexico to the Canadian West.

And yet, in my view, there is the possibility such a scenario may not come to pass. In twenty or thirty years, when the final crisis of the ninth form takes place, the United States will be weary—weary of power, weary of the ingratitude of those whose security it had guaranteed yet who still considered themselves its victims. It will need to stop and catch breath, to look after its own, to restore its finances, dress its wounds, improve the well-being of its own people, huddle over their preoccupations, and above all defend itself on its own soil. It will no longer want to run the risk of having a war at home. It will no longer attempt to manage a world now out of range of its finances, its troops, and its diplomacy. Its armies will become essentially defensive. Indeed, at this moment, the leaders in Washington can justify the continued presence of American troops abroad only by invoking the need to defend the national territory and protect American citizens.

America will remain a very great power. But by choice—and not from weariness or under external constraint—it will no longer be either the dominant empire or the core of the mercantile order.

It is obviously difficult to give a more accurate date to this renunciation, unless it is history's warning that the life span of empires is increasingly short. The Roman Empire of the East lasted 1,058 years; the Holy Roman Empire, 1,006 years; the empires of the East, four hundred years apiece; the Chinese empires, less than three centuries; the Dutch empire, two and a half centuries; the British Empire, a century; the Soviet empire, seventy years; the Japanese, German, and Italian bids for empire, even less. The United States, the dominant empire for the last 120 years—already longer than the average for the most recent empires—will soon cease to dominate the world.

This prospect may seem inconceivable to many. Today, a majority of American leaders still think that the American empire will be eternal. Besides, for them America is a democracy, not an empire. It is invested with a redemptive mission on a planetary scale; these leaders behave as if time (in other words God) could do nothing except serve their interests—as though America, invulnerable and beyond reproach, were still to be mistress of the world several centuries from now. Many people around it in the rest of the world (including some of its worst adversaries) believe it, too. It makes no difference. Within three decades we must search elsewhere for the world's new core.

Other sites suggest themselves. History has taught us that a core does not need to be located on the territory of the very biggest or most densely populated nation in order to aspire to that status. Bruges was not, nor were Venice and the cities that succeeded them. To reach their position, they had to find within themselves the energy, the creative power, the urge to innovate, to mass-produce, to expose themselves to the world, to dominate. By these criteria, several cities could come forward as candidates within twenty or thirty years.

London, first of all, would possess the means. The European continent's leading financial center, a pole of attraction for the world's elites and at the same time close to two of the greatest universities in the world, in twenty or thirty years London will still retain many of the characteristics of a core: a diverse population, an exceptional port and airports, and peerless creative capacity. But this will not be enough; the city that was the core in the nineteenth century will no longer possess the industrial hinterland or the infrastructure of transport and public services essential to production of future consumer articles. The City of London will be no more than a formidable financial platform, at once sophisticated and fragile: it could be forsaken at the slightest technological or military uncertainty, and many who live there now will flee it at the next explosion of the housing bubble.

The core could also be put together athwart the

vast conurbation built in Europe along the whole line of high-speed trains, from London to Frankfurt via Brussels, Lille, and Paris, which offers both the financial and the industrial power required. This would perhaps be possible if the political, industrial, and military integration of certain countries of the European Union, including France and Germany, were far enough advanced to have created a strong political, industrial and military power — without which a core would be hard-pressed to sustain its role. This region could then replace California, and the euro could perhaps replace the dollar. But this will probably not occur, in any case not before powerful shocks and aftershocks, which will happen much later, and which we shall discuss in the following chapters. It would in fact require this will to exist, to lead, to go forward together, to gather in talents from elsewhere, this urge to take power over the world, stimulated by fear of want and the courage to risk one's life and soul that have shaped all the cores. But these qualities no longer seem to have a reason to exist without the stimulus of terrible threats, threats that will come later in this part of Europe.

Another core could emerge in the Scandinavian countries, between Stockholm, Helsinki, and Oslo. There we can find (and will find more and more) exceptionally relaxed human relationships, state-of-the-art industries, excellent universities, major petroleum resources, high educational levels, great security, and outstanding social protection. The region also offers a high quality of life, which, paradoxically, will be further improved by climate warming — even as that same climatic effect threatens the coastlines. But in my opinion the

Nordic countries, anxious to protect themselves from the world's dangers, will refuse to meddle in others' affairs except as clandestine diplomats, not anxious to attract the attention of freedom's enemies. So they will reject the role of core — for a core is never neutral.

No other city and no other country in Europe will be ready to meet the costs for protection and expansion of a core. The role is therefore not close to crossing the Atlantic a second time.

Tokyo would be another serious candidate. Around 2030 its industries will possess a certain advance over those of the other Asian countries of the Pacific rim, and will play a major part in the conception of future objects. But the Japanese capital was unable to seize its chance in the 1980s, and in 2030 will still fail to create universal values: individual freedom is not its philosophical ideal. Nor will it be able to attract enough foreign talent. Besides, in the absence of reconciliation with China and Korea, Japan will still be unable to assume the role of political protector of outlying countries and the hinterland — and still less to assume the planetary military role incumbent on a core.

In about 2030, two other Asian cities, Bombay and Shanghai, will be the leading cities in the world's biggest economies. They also might aspire to become this core of the mercantile order. They will both in fact be major ports, receiving the products of an immense hinterland and importing whatever comes in from the rest of the world. But to have the opportunity of becoming this core they will have to possess the ability to create communications networks, as well as urban, legislative, police, military, and technological infrastructures. They must be able to stabilize their political environment and find the jobs essential for managing an overspilling rural population. As I see it, both these cities will fail, at least over the next three decades. Too busy dealing with their internal problems, faced with the threat of having to confront the rebellions of other less privileged provinces, lacking the most elementary infrastructures, they will not be ready in time to take over the torch from the ninth form.

Australia will doubtless also be ready — in the distant future — to become a core. It is a second America, possessing the same dynamic and the same ability to welcome immigrants, possessing the same will to develop the technologies of the future, and even blessed — today — with one of the world's very best ports. But it is still too sparsely populated, too isolated from the rest of the world. It would need to make enormous progress in the transport of goods to put Sydney less than two hours' flight from Los Angeles or Tokyo, as against five days by ship. And it would need a population of at least 100 million. All this would seem to be beyond its reach for many years to come.

Russia and Canada, their climates improved by global warming, will nevertheless not be credible aspirants. Islam too will dream of welcoming the core, whether in Cairo, Ankara, Baghdad, or Jakarta. But in 2035 it will be far from having the industrial, financial, cultural, and political means. For that, it would need an intellectual freedom unimaginable today.

It is also conceivable that the core might topple over into the virtual universe and that virtual automata will reign. We shall return to this.

Finally, it is rather tempting to think that the migration of cores will continue westward, pursuing the voyage begun three thousand years ago, and moving successively through Japan, China, Australia, and India, finally ending up one day in the Middle East where the mercantile order was conceived. One could even imagine the core stopping in Jerusalem, now capital of all the states in the region, finally at peace with one another. Even a world city — why not? — the planetary capital of all market democracies, or capital of a planetary market democracy. But Jerusalem doesn't have the other prerequisites for being a core.

While awaiting the advent of this very distant utopia (which we shall discuss later, in the third wave of the future), no core seems likely to take over from Los Angeles. For a very long period of time, until the following waves of the future unfurl, a core will no longer be necessary to the functioning of the order. The market will have become powerful enough and the costs of data exchange low enough to free the members of the innovative class of the need to live in the same place in order to rule the world. New industry will be born in a thousand sites at a time: the mercantile form will function without a core.

Capitalism will be all the more thriving — more dynamic, more promising, more dominant. Those who have announced its funeral will once again regret their words.

4

First Wave of the Future: Planetary Empire

In the United States and elsewhere, many predict that history will henceforth relate nothing at all but the spread of markets, then of democracy, within the frontiers of each country — in other words, the End of History. This evolution, they say, will take place naturally and peacefully. According to them, it will not require a war of democracies against the last dictatorships: it was not by bombing Moscow that we could wash our hands of the Soviet Union, nor by bombing and occupying Baghdad that we shall "democratize" Iraq. Nor is there any need for recourse to economic sanctions: no embargo, they argue, has ever defeated a single dictatorship. The peoples of the world, they hope, will free themselves simply through the workings of economic growth, transparency of information, and the expansion of the middle classes. They predict that the mercantile order will then be polycentric, in other words a juxtaposition of a growing number of market democracies around a few dominant powers.

Such a scenario will certainly come about. Between 2025 and 2035, while the ninth form is fading away, it will give place to a masterless world, tenuously coordinated by a handful of powers. But I do not believe this can last. A completely different world, working in the direct line dictated by history, will then take its place—a market without democracy.

In about 2050, harried by the pressure of market demands and thanks to new technological means, the world order will coalesce around a market that has become planetary—and stateless. There will begin what I shall call super-empire, deconstructing public services, then sovereign states, and then the very nations themselves.

This global market, unified and stateless, will long remain faithful to the values of the former Californian core. And since London's cultural values long resembled Amsterdam's, Boston's those of London, and those of Los Angeles resembled New York's, the super-empire will remain partially American. As we shall see, its consumer items will be very largely an extension of nomadic items, just like its culture (hybrid), its way of life (precarious), its values (individualist), and its ideal (narcissistic).

Thus will begin the first phase of the future. Then, as we shall see, may* come a series of wars, leading to hyperconflict. And finally, faced with the failure of super-empire and of hyperconflict, new values will lead to readjustment on a global scale of the balance between democracy and market—and to a planetary hyper-democracy.

---

*Note I say "may," for my fervent hope, and one of the goals of this book, is to paint the near future, the next hundred years, forcefully and convincingly enough to render war impossible. But history has shown us that too many wars—however senseless they may seem in retrospect—have occurred to ignore their possibility.

The Spread of Market Democracy: A Polycentric World

Wherever it is still not the case (essentially China and the Muslim world), sometime around 2035 commercial growth will create a middle class that overthrows dictatorship and brings a parliamentary democracy into being.

From there we shall continue to witness, as we have done for two centuries, the universalization — progressive and parallel, chaotic, and irreversible — of the market and then of democracy. This phenomenon will even carry with it Egypt, Indonesia, Nigeria, Congo, China, and Iran. Intact or in little pieces, all these countries will be swept away by the logic that once swept away dictatorship in Chile, Spain, Russia, and Turkey. Islam, Hinduism, and Confucianism will no longer oppose democracy. Indeed, each of these ancient wisdoms will even claim parental rights to democracy.

The organization of free elections will obviously not be enough for the long-term establishment of market democracies. The Iraqi, Algerian, or Zimbabwean examples show that even free elections — if they are unaccompanied by stable economic and political institutions, and if the citizens show no true desire to live together — can on the contrary force democracy to retreat. These countries must (as all the others before them have done) equip themselves progressively with secular constitutions, parliaments, political parties, judicial and police systems working in full respect for human rights, and a genuine plurality in information. It will take them time: we must not demand of Asia and Africa what nobody at the time demanded of Europe.

To help them, the already democratic nations must deploy their own values and institutions and not their missiles. They must open their markets to the businesses, the products, and the students from these countries. They must finance job-creating investments there, encourage the emergence of modern farming methods, a banking system, social security, a judicial and police system, and finally promote newspapers, radio networks, new elites, and nongovernmental organizations.

In the course of this process, tribal groups, regions, and peoples will decide not to go on living with one another. Wealthy regions will rid themselves of the burden of poor regions, as was the case when the Czech Republic sundered itself from Slovakia. Among existing democracies, Flanders could opt to separate from Wallonia, northern Italy from the south, Catalonia from the rest of Spain, as Scotland could claim independence from the United Kingdom. The Kurds might dissociate themselves from other Iraqis, and the Indians and the Indonesians could even decide to distance themselves from each other. The states artificially created during the colonial era in Africa or Asia could also burst asunder. More than a hundred new nations could be born before the end of the century.

In each of these future democracies, as in the old ones, a growing share of the national revenue will briefly be handled by public budgets and by insurance systems, social or private, which will usher in mutual benefit insurance for health risks and for those related to aging. This process will go hand in hand with the progressive disappearance of the peasant and worker class and swift rise of the middle classes—less acquainted with the harsher aspects of toil, and in a better position to satisfy themselves with formal freedoms and material well-being.

For as long as democracy and market remain equal powers, they will share their areas of competence and respect the borders between them. The mercantile order will organize itself as a juxtaposition of market democracies; the world will be polycentric, with one or two major powers on each continent—the United States, Brazil, Russia, and the European Union, even if the last-named will not offer all the attributes of a state. Nigeria, the most populated country, will join them if it still exists, which seems unlikely. Together, these nine nations, mistresses of the polycentric order, will constitute an informal world government, which I shall return to in the third wave of the future. We shall see them again at the Security Council and at meetings of the G8.

Such a polycentric order will be unable to hold together. By its nature, the market is a conqueror: it accepts no limits, shares no territory, and engages in no truces. It will not sign a peace treaty with states. It will refuse to leave them any competencies. It will soon reach into all public services and will drain governments (even those of the masters of the polycentric order) of their last prerogatives, including those of sovereignty.

Even if nations, regulatory agencies, and international organizations briefly seek to contain and limit the markets, industrial, financial, and technological powers (whether legal or illegal) will refuse to accept any kind of polycentric balance. They will butt constantly against frontiers and compete with all the public services, one after another. Then the education and health services and those linked to the exercise of sovereignty will cease entirely to be public: doctors, teachers, then judges and soldiers will become salary-earners of the private sector.

Finally, like others before them, these services—now become too costly in time and money because of the aging of the planet, of massive urbanization, of growing insecurity, of the ecological stakes, and of the need to train oneself permanently—will be replaced by mass-produced industrial objects.

Now will begin (it has already begun) a colossal geopolitical battle for planetary supremacy between market democracies and the market. This battle will lead to the victory—unthinkable today—of capitalism over the United States, and even of the market over democracy. Here is its story.

The Object as Substitute for the State: From Hypersurveillance to Self-Surveillance

The markets will progressively find new sources of profitability in activities that are today exercised by the public services: education, health, environment, sovereignty. Private enterprises will seek first to commercialize these services, then replace them with mass-produced consumer objects, dovetailing perfectly with the dynamic of technical progress at work since the beginnings of the mercantile order.

First they will seek (and find) new means of accumulating more and more energy and information in increasingly reduced spaces—in particular to diminish consumption of energy, raw materials, and water, and face the consequences for the environment. This will take place through the use of technologies permitting storage of energy and information on nanometric entities (whence the term nanotechnologies). We shall move toward the construction of nanomachines by assembling molecules, which will require locating, manipulating, and positioning atoms. Diverse technologies will make it possible to economize on water, forests, and petroleum, and to use still uncertain resources like the wealth of the oceans and of space. Microprocessors will use DNA and peptide biomolecules, which will serve in the construction of nanocomputers. Nanoenergy power stations will work on hydrogen batteries. Autoresponders will be capable of repairing and reproducing themselves. In addition, major technical advances will improve the ecological effectiveness of materials, of propulsion, aerodynamics, structures, combustibles, motors, and systems.

These technologies will radically transform the way in which current objects are produced. They will allow the consumption of much less energy per unit produced, better management of drinking water, urban wastes, and polluting emissions. They will improve the characteristics of food products, clothing, housing, vehicles, household equipment, and nomadic objects.

Other nomadic objects — such as lenses, glasses, and prostheses of different kinds — will miniaturize the means of information, entertainment, communication, and transport, leading to a massive rise in nomadic ubiquity. The single nomadic object will be integrated one way or another into the body. It will serve as a sensor and a controller. Adapted plastic materials, reusable and recyclable, will allow the transformation of clothing into linked nomadic objects. Other plastic materials will become throwaway screens, allowing for creation of wall-pictures in public places and in connected households. This will turn our way of lighting, building, reading, and living on its head. Personalized robots will help the sick and then the healthy in their daily lives. Robots will allow simultaneous participation in several virtual meetings and the reproduction, at least virtual, of a vanished or fantasized person. Self-steering cars will relieve us of the need to drive, at least on the freeway. Hypersonic aircraft will put Los Angeles less than four hours from any point in the Pacific; ships will put every Asian port less than twenty-four hours from one another and will reduce transpacific runs to three days. Diverse private companies will send tourists to hotels in space and organize voyages to the moon, and later to Mars.

Around 2040 the essential will begin. It will cut massively into the cost of organizing market democracies, reestablishing the profitability of industry, gradually reducing the role of states to zero, and destroying, little by little, the polycentric order. Acting as the engines of growth, new objects will take over from automobiles, washing machines, and nomadic objects: these will be surveillance objects, replacing many traditionally state-run functions. I shall call them the Watchers.

Services such as education, health, and sovereignty will thus be slowly replaced — as was the case with transport, domestic services, and communication — by mass-produced machines. This will once again open new markets for businesses and raise the profitability of the economy. Since this will mean manipulation of services essential to social order — indeed the foundation stones of states and peoples — it will radically modify relations with the individual or collective imagination, with identity, life, sovereignty, knowledge, power, nation, culture, and geopolitics.

And now we stand before the most sweeping revolution awaiting us in the next half century.

These Watchers will not spring forth ready-made from the imagination of crazed researchers or technicians touched by the hand of God. They will be responding to the financial imperatives of the mercantile order, always on the lookout for new ways to reduce the time needed to produce existing objects, to raise network capacities, reduce collective expenses, enhance the use of time, and transform desires and needs into commercial wealth.

This process will go through two stages, which I shall call *hypersurveillance* and *self-surveillance.*

When the law of the market starts to prevail over that of democracies, public services (education, health care, security, and then justice and sovereignty) will begin to face competition from private enterprise. States will be expected to treat chains of foreign hospitals as public hospitals, and the affiliates of foreign private universities as national universities.

Private security, police, and information will compete with national police forces in surveillance of movement and data, on behalf of insurance and commercial companies. These will want to know everything about their employees, clients, suppliers, competitors, and risks; they will also want to protect their assets, material, financial, and intellectual, against a range of threats. This transfer to the private sector will gradually reduce public spending and help save on scarce resources. As we have already seen, it will become part and parcel of the host of services making it possible to track objects and people. Nomadic ubiquity opens itself to hypersurveillance when whoever is connected leaves traces of his passage.

Private services will then manage social rights and the administrative services. We will be in a position to receive an administrative document or an allotment by paying more: this is already the case with Great Britain. In many places the state is henceforth relieved of the burden of countless decisions, entrusted to high independent authorities that relieve the state of all responsibility.

To put it in different terms: in exchange for a tax cut that will above all benefit the wealthiest (and penalize the poorest), we shall henceforth have to pay for public services. And since these competing private enterprises will have to spend considerable sums to attract clients — which a public service does not have to do — the service's final cost for the client will rise accordingly.

Users (private individuals or businesses) will become consumers, obliged to pay directly for their services, whether in the form of a direct purchase from providers or else in the form of premiums paid to insurance companies (private or public) as a substitute for tax revenue, which will plummet.

These insurance companies will demand not only that their clients pay their premiums (to insure themselves against sickness, joblessness, death, theft, fire, insecurity) but will also verify that their clients conform to norms to minimize the risks they will be called on to cover. They will gradually come to dictate planetary norms (What to eat? What to know? How to drive? How to protect oneself? How to consume? How to produce?). They will penalize smokers, drinkers, the obese, the unemployable, the inadequately protected, the aggressive, the careless, the clumsy, the absentminded, the spendthrift. Ignorance, exposure to risks, wasting, and vulnerability will be considered diseases. Other businesses will also have to comply with norms in order to avoid industrial disasters, work accidents, or external aggression, and even the wastage of real resources. In a certain way, all businesses will thus be forced to take account of the general interest in making their decisions. Some will even make their "citizenship" a dimension of their image and their competence.

The rise of risks linked to aging, to urban growth, to disasters triggered by ecological disturbances, and to terrorist attacks will gradually raise the share of these insurance premiums in the national revenue, at the same time as the share of obligatory tax and social security contributions will go down.

Businesses will have at once to respect the norms imposed on them by the insurance companies, and in their turn require their collaborators — a part of whose contribution they will pay — to comply with other norms. This compliance will imply monitoring one's health, knowledge, vigilance, and property. Being thrifty with rare resources, keeping an eye on one's health, training, and protecting oneself (and more generally *staying in shape*) will become socially necessary behaviors.

For the insurance companies to pay off economically, everyone — private individual or business — must therefore agree that a third party verify his conformity with the norms. For this, everyone must agree to be monitored. The era of Big Brother, earlier proclaimed but only partially implemented, will become the norm.

"Surveillance": Masterword for the Times Ahead

First of all, a kind of hypersurveillance will see the light of day. Technology will make it possible to know everything about the origins of products and movements of men — which will much later imply essential military applications. Sensors and miniature cameras installed in all public (and eventually private) places, in offices and in recreational areas, and finally on the nomadic objects themselves, will monitor all comings and goings (the phone already allows us to communicate and be tracked). Biometric techniques — fingerprints, iris, shape of hands and face — will allow for surveillance of travelers, workers, and consumers. Countless analytical devices will make it possible to monitor the health of a body, a mind, or a product.

The unique nomadic object will be permanently traceable. All the data it contains, including images of everyone's daily life, will be stored and sold to specialist businesses and to public and private police. Individual data on health and competence will be updated by private databases that will allow for predictive tests in view of preventive treatment. Prison — already a heavy financial burden to most nation-states — will be gradually replaced by long-distance surveillance of a person under house arrest.

Nothing will be hidden anymore. Discretion, hitherto a condition of social life, will no longer have a raison d'être. Everyone will know everything about everybody, and we shall evolve in the direction of less guilt and more tolerance. Forgetfulness was yesterday tinged with remorse, but tomorrow transparency will encourage us to do without it. Curiosity, based on a culture of secrecy, will also disappear — to the dismay of scandal sheets. Celebrity will go the same way.

A little later, around 2050, the market will no longer be satisfied with organizing long-distance surveillance: mass-produced objects will allow everyone to monitor his own compliance with the norms, and self-surveillance will appear. Machines will permit everyone, public or private, to monitor his own consumption of energy, water, raw materials, and so forth, while other machines will offer self-surveillance of his or her savings and inheritance. These machines will also help save time for living. Already the mirror, scales, thermometer, alcohol tests, pregnancy tests, electrocardiograms, and countless sensors are measuring parameters, comparing them to a value self-styled normal, and announcing the test results to the world. New technologies will arise to multiply these portable means of surveillance. Computers will be integrated into clothing by nanofibers and will miniaturize still further the body's self-monitors. Electronic bugs, worn subcutaneously, will ceaselessly register heartbeat, blood pressure, and cholesterol. Microprocessors connected to various organs will watch their functioning as compared to the norms. Miniature cameras, electronic sensors, biomarkers, nanomotors, and nanotubes (microscopic sensors that can be introduced into the pulmonary alveola or the bloodstream) will give everyone the opportunity to measure, permanently or periodically, the parameters of his own body.

On matters of education and information, we shall also see the appearance of self-surveillance instruments and software for monitoring compliance with the norms related to knowledge. They will organize verification of acquaintances. The nomadic ubiquity of information will become the permanent monitor for knowledge.

For a little longer, only doctors and teachers (working together on production and testing of these self-surveillance devices) will be authorized to use them. Then these objects will be miniaturized, simplified, manufactured at extremely low cost, and made available to all, despite the stern opposition of the experts with whom they will enter into competition. Surveillance will become nomadic and ubiquitous. Everyone will return with passion to these instruments. Fear of physical deterioration and of ignorance, growing familiarity with nomadic objects, mistrust of the medical and educational guilds, and faith in technological infallibility will open enormous markets for this variegated spectrum of devices. Bent on establishing continual adjustments to their premiums on evaluation of the risks run by each of their clients, insurance companies will urge them to participate in the markets. They will therefore insist that their clients furnish proof that they use self-surveillance.

Practitioners will then find themselves a new niche treating diseases that would not have been detected earlier, while teachers will become tutors to those singled out as refractory in the knowledge field.

Once again, collective services (this time state-run) will become mass-produced industrial products. Everything put in place over the last several decades will meet a triumphant conclusion. Everyone will now have become his own prison guard. And at the same time, individual freedom will have reached the mountaintop—at least in the imagination, by the use of new nomadic objects.

Beyond the *self-monitors* will come (are already coming) *self-repairers*, making it possible to correct mistakes detected by the self-monitors. One of the early forms of this self-repair will have been the makeup, beauty, fashion, fitness, and cosmetic surgery industries. The aging of the world will create greater need for them. It will begin with the integration of self-repair equipment into artificial systems such as machines, bridges, buildings, cars, household equipment, and nomadic objects. Then microprocessors (first built with organic materials and later from biomaterials) will focus on repairing bodies. They will deliver medication at regular intervals: microcapsules will be introduced into the blood with the mission of detecting and repairing the beginnings of a cancer and to combat the aging of brain and body. If we come to know the genetic mechanisms of alcohol or drug dependency we may also try to block the behaviors they trigger. It will even be possible one day to manipulate the interior of cells without damaging them in order to repair human organs in vivo.

And still further ahead, advances in the neurosciences will allow us to go in search (through a purely mental act) of acquaintances and information stored in external databases, without the prior obligation to store them in our own memory. Bionic prostheses directly connected to the brain will help us build bridges between spheres of knowledge, produce mental images, travel, learn, fantasize, and communicate with other minds. We can already move a cursor on a screen thanks to a mental image transmitted to a computer through the workings of an electronic implant in the motor cortex. This already allows a quadriplegic to write fifteen words a minute through a simple thought transmission, and to send them off by e-mail. Telepathy is thus (already) reality. Tomorrow, these processes will make it possible to come up with new forms of direct communication via the mind and improve the process of apprenticeship and onscreen network creation. They will also become a source of new artistic sensations.

The Deconstruction of Nation-States

These technologies will make themselves felt at a time when the costs of public services become heavier and heavier. Country by country, sector by sector, they will progressively reduce the role of the state and the public institutions for provisions for the future. Thus, after rising, the share of collective expenses in the national revenue of each country will fall disastrously.

Growth of markets in the polycentric world will then work in the same direction as these technologies and will themselves contribute to the massive weakening of states. First of all, the great corporations, with a base of thousands of specialist companies, will bring influence to bear on the media (using advertising to blackmail them) in order to orient citizens' choices.

In an early phase, when wealthy minorities realize that they have more to gain by putting a property on the market than by putting it to the vote, they will do everything to have that property privatized. Thus, for example, when a rich minority thinks that the retirement system by allocation is no longer in line with its interests, it will shift it (by initiating short-lived alliances) into a system of retirement by capitalization — so that its pensions will no longer depend on a majority decision that might prove unfavorable to it. The same will be true for health, police, education, and the environment.

Then the market, by nature planetary, will violate/breach the laws of democracy, by nature local. The wealthiest members of the innovative class (a few hundred million among the two billion holders of shares, of mobile assets, and of mobile knowledge) will consider their sojourn in any country (including that of their birthplace — even if that were one of the masters of the polycentric order) as an individual contract excluding all loyalty and all solidarity with their compatriots. They will exile themselves if they feel they have not gotten their money's worth.

Similarly, when businesses (including those of nations now mistresses of the polycentric order) decide that the tax code and the law applicable to them are not the best they might wish for, they will relocate their decision-making centers outside their country of origin.

States will then compete with one another by announcing massive cuts in taxes on capital and on the innovative class—which will gradually deprive them of the bulk of their resources. Utterly drained, and pushed as well by the appearance of self-surveillance devices, states will abandon to the market the task of proposing the bulk of services related to education, health, security, and even sovereignty. They will do it first by relocating public services to countries with a low-cost labor force, and next by privatizing them. Then taxes will go down and the minimum wage statutes, as well as statutes for the protection of the weakest, will be swept away. Financial insecurity will become the rule for everyone.

In the absence of a state, businesses will increasingly favor consumers over workers—whose incomes will go down. Self-surveillance technologies will organize and accelerate this process by favoring the consumer over the user of public services, profit over wages, while giving increasing power to insurance and entertainment companies and to self-surveillance producers.

Then, by 2050 at the latest, a slow deconstruction of states—some of them born more than a thousand years ago—will begin. The middle class, the leading player in market democracy, will rediscover the insecurity it believed it had escaped by detaching itself from the working class. Contract will increasingly win out over law, mercenaries over armies and police forces, and arbitrators over judges. Jurists specializing in private law will have a field day.

For a time, states belonging to countries that are masters of the polycentric order will still be able to control a few rules of their social life. In such states, those politically of age will join forces with their economic counterparts—in other words, the age at which the child becomes an autonomous consumer. In each country, utterly confused political parties will seek (more and more vainly) for areas of competence. Neither left nor right will be able to prevent the progressive privatization of education, health, security, insurance, nor the replacement of these services by mass-produced objects—nor, a little later, the dawning of super-empire. The right will even accelerate this advent with privatizations. The left will do the same, by giving the middle class the means to access (more equitably) the marketing of time and to private consumption. Public expropriation of big corporations will no longer be a credible solution. Social movements will no longer have the strength to oppose the marketing of the world. Mediocre governments, leaning on the few remaining civil servants and on discredited parliamentarians and manipulated by pressure groups, will continue to put on shows rarely visited and less and less taken seriously. Public opinion will not show much more interest in their deeds and gestures than they show today in the deeds and gestures of the very last monarchs on the European continent.

Nations will be nothing more than oases competing with one another to attract passing caravans. Their way of life will be limited by the rare resources brought by the few nomads who agree to make a halt there long enough to produce, trade, and entertain themselves. Countries will no longer be lived in at any length by anyone but the sedentary—forced to be there because they are too hostile to risk, too fragile, too young, or too old—and by the weakest, some of them immigrants from elsewhere in search of a more decent way of life.

The only states to pursue development will be those

that have attracted the loyalty of their citizens by favoring their creativity, their successful integration, and their social mobility. Some nations in the social-democratic tradition and some tiny state-run entities will resist better than others. Irony of history: with the advent of super-empire, we shall witness the return of those city-states that dominated the beginnings of the mercantile order.

To prevent this destruction of national identity and stand up to the immigrant waves that will follow, racist dictators (whether theocratic or secular) will seize power in certain states. What will soon play out, particularly in countries like the Netherlands or Belgium (the first cores of the mercantile world, and among the planet's most ancient democracies), will be revelatory of the evolution that next settles on the most robust states (and on those most concerned about their freedoms).

While Africa vainly struggles to construct itself, the rest of the world will begin to deconstruct itself under the hammer-blows of globalization. Tomorrow's Africa will therefore not resemble today's West. Rather, it is tomorrow's West that will resemble today's Africa.

And then (in my opinion even before the twenty-first century ends) the government of the United States will itself lose — doubtless the last in the bosom of this polycentric world — the essentials of its instruments of sovereignty.

This will happen first in the virtual world. As we have seen, the printing press once acted against the powers that be. In the same way, the Internet will act against the United States. It will begin by not serving Washington's interests. Then, playing on its free-of-charge services, multiplying its information sources, liberating the controls imposed on information by the wealthier, it will drain the U.S. government (like that of the other countries) of many of its most important powers. Many people will even claim citizenship of the virtual universe, abandoning citizenship of every real state, even that of the United States.

In the real world, businesses of American origin will relocate their research centers and their headquarters, thus depriving the federal American state of the bulk of its resources. Financing the many functions of sovereignty, in particular of defense, will be more and more onerous. And finally, the citizenry will no longer want to see its children die in battle, and will no longer want to be forced to take part in the defense of its country.

Certain forces, especially military, will then attempt to restore the means of action to the federal state by nationalizing strategic businesses, closing the borders, and squaring up, if necessary, to former allies. The means of information will lie and attempt to dress up an increasingly inaccessible reality. In vain. On its last legs, Washington will have to relinquish control of the great economic and political decisions to each state of the Union and to the big corporations. Administrative services will be privatized one after the other. Prisons will become private businesses with zero labor costs. Even the army, the last refuge of sovereignty, will eventually be privatized like all the rest.

Then, like the Roman Empire in its day, the American empire will disappear without leaving a political authority in place in the new Rome. States and nations will still have a place — nostalgic apparitions, fleeting ghosts, scapegoats both impotent and easy to direct in the absolute marketing of time.

The Absolute Marketing of Time

Capitalism will then march to its end, destroying everything that is not itself. It will transform the world into an immense market, its destiny disconnected from that of nations and freed from the demands and the servitude of a core. Like the American empire before it and like each of the nine forms of the mercantile order, this super-empire will carry an extraordinary message of freedom, but it will also have extremely alienating dimensions. It will put the finishing touches to what the market had begun since its origins — making every minute of life an opportunity to produce, to trade, or to consume mercantile goods.

Like the conquerors of the Roman Empire, the markets will hasten to don the garments of the vanquished: American society will long remain the model the super-empire proposes to the world. Super-empire will also urge businesses to enter every surveillance market. It will urge every student to finance his own advanced studies and his permanent training. To defend the private ownership of belongings, ideas, patents, and persons in the absence of a state, but also to protect the environment, the market will produce police forces, armies, private jurisdiction, mercenaries, and arbitrators.

All time spent on anything but consuming — or on accumulating consumer objects in a different way — will be considered lost. The market will go so far as to dissolve headquarters, factories, and workshops so that people may start consuming as soon as they leave their houses, working, playing, staying informed, learning, and self-monitoring. Upper limits on retirement age will vanish. People will work, if they can, without constraint. Transportation will become centers of commerce. Hospitals and schools will essentially give place to sales areas and to after-sale services for self-surveillance and self-repair units, which will become (as we shall see) the seeds of the third wave of the future.

The more solitary a man is, the more he will consume, and then he will monitor and distract himself in order to furnish his solitude. Individual freedom, constantly increased (in appearance at least) by self-monitoring, will lead everyone to consider himself responsible for his own private sphere, both professional and private, to obey (in appearance) only his own whim, and in reality to comply with the norms setting the requirements for his own survival.

We have seen how the nomad of man's earliest societies, like the citizen of market democracies, obeyed a body of complex rules, the expression of multiple collective ambitions. But the citizen of super-empire will no longer be bound by the slightest social contract. In a situation of nomadic ubiquity, tomorrow's man — and woman — will perceive the world as a totality at his or her service — within the limits of norms imposed by the insurance companies on his or her individual behavior. He will see the Other as a tool of his own happiness, a means of procuring pleasure or money or even both for himself. No one will dream of concerning himself with other people. Why share when you must fight? Why work in unison when you are competitors? No one will think any longer that the happiness of someone else might be useful to him. Still less will he think of seeking his happiness in that of the other. Any collective action will seem unthinkable—and therefore all political change inconceivable.

Solitude will begin with childhood. No one can force parents, whether biological or adoptive, to respect and love their children long enough to raise them. Precocious grown-ups, the youngest will suffer from a solitude no longer compensated by any of the networks of previous societies. Likewise, more and more of the elderly, living longer and thus alone for longer than in the past, will one day know practically no one among the living. By then, the world will be no more than a juxtaposition of solitudes, and love a juxtaposition of masturbations.

To combat this solitude, many at any age will choose to share with others, temporarily or permanently, a roof, goods, advantages, fights, games, even in the absence of any shared sex life, in any case without obligation to faithfulness, and accepting the multiplicity of their respective partners. In these networks, many will seek endless opportunities for risky encounters, whether remunerated or not. They will find substitutes for their solitude in self-surveillance objects and self-repair drugs.

To manage mercantile time, the two dominant industries will still be insurance and distraction. Insurance companies (and the risk-coverage institutions of the financial markets) will create private police forces that will first take care of hypersurveillance of businesses, consumers, and workers. They will spend considerable sums to shape public opinion and gain the loyalty of their clients. They will require of them the obligation to respect the norms, and then the purchase of self-surveillance items. For the poorest, microinsurance will no longer be (as it was in the ninth form) an instrument for promoting democracy but its substitute. Similarly, the distraction industries will use surveillance technologies and offer performances ceaselessly adapted to the reactions of the spectators, whose emotions will be permanently captured, monitored, and integrated into the play. The fact that the spectacle will be free of charge will serve as a support for new consumption. In order not to seem reduced to fear management, self-surveillance will dress itself up as information, as a game, or as entertainment. What remains of politics will also become a pure stage-managed show put on by politicians, occasional players in a neglected performance.

Nomadic Businesses

By 2020, in other words well before super-empire overthrows nations, many businesses will begin to do without sedentary bases. They will be either temporary groupings of individuals or else permanent gatherings of tribes. In either case, they will be in ferocious competition with one another to win over clients and investors.

The first, structured on the lines of a theatrical troupe, will assemble (they are already doing so) the skills and the capital to fulfill a determined task. Their longevity will depend on the projects of those who founded them, on their ability to invent new products, and on the decisions of their financiers and their clients. Since people's life expectancy will have risen considerably, these businesses will endure for much less time than those who work in them. Most of them will disappear at the very latest with their creators: their employees will be temporaries, hired to do a given job. Their work, under increasing constraint from the requirements of profitability, of the just-in-time, of the made-to-measure, will be more and more stress-inducing, flexible, and insecure. These "troupes" (businesses) will play in "theaters" (the markets awaiting them) for as long as they have "spectators" (clients). They will disperse after putting on a "play" (a product) or several plays. Microbusinesses will construct the essentials of these "theatrical companies." Many will be tiny multinationals, made up of a few associates located anywhere on the planet. As always, creative work will be the chief source of wealth.

Much rarer, businesses of the second category will be organized over the long haul on the lines of circuses or movie studios, in other words around a name, a story, a project. They will assemble several troupes (temporary employees, continually replaced by others). They will perform in places that change constantly, places where the market is to be found. The public will be drawn in by the past fame of the circus, and will come to consume its products without prior knowledge—although they should have precise knowledge of the "theater's" products before visiting it. Their all-important quality will be the ability to select the shows they will put on every season. Their cultures, languages, and whereabouts will be mobile and unpredictable. Their administrative boards will be made up of very well-paid governance professionals. Their leaders will need time to think over the long term in order to find new attractions in advance: they will have to manage flexible production processes, local marketing teams, and targeted marketing campaigns with teams specializing in worldwide coordination. They will have to do all they can to develop the creativity of their fellow workers (even temporary workers), and the loyalty of their clients (even occasional clients).

These firms will in fact be fitters, "props assistants" bringing together modules manufactured by specialized subcontractors, themselves "theatrical troupes" in pitiless competition with one another. They will essentially be networks of nomadic associates. To keep those of their collaborators they value, they will offer them everything a state once did: from lifestyle to security, from insurance to training. Their chief asset will be their brand name, which they will protect and sustain to keep consumers eager for their future products. They will finance vast communications programs in order to constitute the right references for a particular universe. They will incarnate values each consumer would like to embody, places everyone will want to visit. They will take environmental and social values into account, thus partly replacing functions abandoned by governments, at the very least by generously funding nongovernmental organizations. The top "circuses" will be industrial firms working in infrastructures, machine tools, motors, food, household equipment, clothing, transport, the tourist industry, distribution, beauty, fitness, entertainment, energy, information, finance, insurance, defense, health, and education. These circuses will establish trademarks and hunt for the best experts to work for them. They will also push ahead in the fields of environment, private security, mercenaries, surveillance, network infrastructures (in particular for finance, urban maintenance, and equipment), environment, transportation, and communication. Huge markets will open more than ever for products destined for the poorest. Microcredit will become more important than the traditional banking system. Insurance companies will acquire the leading "circuses" and will ensure their growth.

Some "circuses" will be bold and intelligent enough to make radical changes in their positioning, as Nokia or General Electric once did.

The leading "circuses" will essentially be of American origin or attached to American values, for it is there that entities best able to assemble the means for a durable global project will be found. We can already name some of them—AIG for insurance, Citigroup for banking, Disney for entertainment, Bechtel for engineering, Whirlpool for household equipment, United Health Group for health, Pearson for education, Wal-Mart for distribution, Exxon for energy, Microsoft for software, Boeing for defense and aviation, Nike for clothing, Coca-Cola for drinks and food. Few will be European: Nokia perhaps, L'Oréal, Nestlé, Danone, Mercedes, Vuitton, HSBC, Sanofi. "Circuses" will next be Indian, Brazilian, Japanese, Chinese, Russian, and Mexican.

Then these firms will sever themselves from a national base and will become totally nomadic. They will endure in general for much longer than financial empires or the investment funds that will briefly own them. Businesses will cease to be hierarchic and will become labyrinthine; they will stop being uniform and will become conglomerates of local businesses, producing made-to-measure goods on request.

Some of these "circuses" will go so far (certain of them are already doing it) as to create their own currency in order to gain the loyalty of their suppliers and their clients. They will do so in the form of "points" given as gifts to their partners. Then they will ensure the transferability of these points outside their own circuits. Soon no one, not even the U.S. government, will be able to oppose them.

If (in a half century or less) insurance companies manage to control the leading businesses and impose their norms on states, if private mercenaries replace armies, if business currencies substitute themselves for the leading world currencies, then super-empire will have won the day.

Faced with enfeebled states, states in their death throes, even states that have vanished into thin air, and faced with the negation of law and the impunity implicit in super-empire, two other categories of business will emerge—*piratical* and *relational.*

First, the businesses the state no longer has the means to ban will reinforce themselves. On the scene since the beginnings of the mercantile order, pirate businesses will see their market broaden. Some will engage in lawful activities without respecting all the laws (particularly fiscal laws). Others will engage in criminal activities (such as the traffic in drugs, arms, human beings, illegal games, influence, money laundering, copies of brand-name products), and will not hesitate to use violence. Their turnover will one day outstrip that of the lawful economy. They will launder their money, some of which will turn up on the legal market, which they will increasingly unsettle. They will even interlock with businesses in the market economy, which they will finance and with which they will establish joint enterprises. To emerge triumphant, they will endow themselves with all the attributes of states on the road to escheat: communications networks, instruments for the collection of resources, arms. They will control the means of information and make of them an instrument of propaganda and of lying on their behalf through fear and corruption. They will endow themselves with microfinance systems, fed on dirty money, to attract and finance the most deprived. They will also be (as we shall see in the next chapter) key players and the initiators of the second wave of the future, that of *hyperconflict*.

Next, reacting against these contradictions in the globalization of trade, businesses with nonlucrative goals, dealing with human relations, will eventually exercise certain of the functions that states can no longer fulfill: the nongovernmental organizations (NGOs) and foundations (both South and North) are already allied with them. By recreating no-cost and voluntary services, they too will imbricate themselves with the market, which will finance them and establish joint enterprises with them. By their very existence, they will give birth to the third wave of the future, hyperdemocracy—where, as we shall see, planetary democratic institutions will contribute to shifting the balance of the super-empire.

Hypernomads: Masters of Super-Empire

The masters of the super-empire will be stars of the "circuses" and of the "theater companies" — holders of the capital of the "circus businesses," financial or business strategists, executives of insurance and leisure companies, software designers, creators, jurists, financiers, authors, designers, artists, creators of nomadic objects. I call them *hypernomads.*

There will be several score millions of them, women as much as men, many self-employed, drifting from "theater" to circus, pitiless competitors, neither employees nor employers, but sometimes filling several jobs at once, managing their lives like a stock portfolio.

Through the workings of a very selective competitive process, they will constitute a new innovative class, a *hyperclass,* which will direct super-empire. They will live in every core of the polycentric world. They will have to defend their title to their capital, their creations, their software, their patents, their tricks of the trade, their receipts, and their works of art. They will speak more and more languages with the help of translating machines. At once hypochondriac, paranoid, and megalomaniac, narcissistic and egocentric, the hypernomads will seek access to the most recent self-monitors and the electronic and chemical drugs delivered by the self-repairers. They will want to live much longer than others. They will experiment with techniques promising them hope of doubling their life span. They will pay homage to every recipe for meditation, relaxation, and for an apprenticeship in self-love.

For them, this apprenticeship will be a vital necessity;

curiosity, an absolute requirement; manipulation, a daily habit. Their aesthetic canons, their distraction, their culture will also be specific. The latter will be more labyrinthine than ever. Their need to model and invent will lead them to banish for themselves the borders between working, consuming, creating, and distancing themselves.

They will thus invent the best and the worst of a volatile, carefree, egotistical, and insecure planetary society. Arbiters of elegance, masters of wealth and the media, they will acknowledge no allegiance, whether national or political or cultural. They will increasingly dress like nomads, their garb recalling their adventures, their prostheses, and their networks. They will be patrons of multiform artists who will mingle forms of virtual art in which emotions are aroused, measured, captured, and modified by the self-monitors. They will live in private cities behind walls guarded by mercenaries. They will cause the price of artworks and real estate to soar.

The couple will no longer be their principal base for life and sexuality. They will prefer to choose, in full transparency, polygamous or polyandrous loves. Men and women, all collectors, more interested in the hunt than the prey, accumulating and exhibiting their trophies, constantly on the move in search of distraction, many of them will be the offspring of mobile families without a geographic or cultural base. They will be loyal only to themselves, and will interest themselves more in their conquests, their wine cellars, their self-monitors, their art collections, and the planning of their erotic lives than in the future of their progeny—to whom they will no longer bequeath either money or power. Nor will they aspire to direct public affairs or to live stage front. In their eyes, celebrity will pass for a curse.

Some of them, more cynical than the others, will serve the pirate economy and become its masters. We will meet them again as lead actors in the second wave of the future.

Others, by contrast, will develop an acute conscience over what is at stake for the planet, and having made their fortunes will invest in humanitarian action. They will become — sometimes just to give themselves a cause to champion — altruists. They will be the inspirers of relational businesses, upholders of a planetary democracy. We shall find them again among the lead players in the third wave of the future.

Like all the other innovative classes before it, this one will exercise a decisive influence on the way of life of those who struggle to imitate it.

Virtual Nomads: From Sports to Live Show

Just below the hypernomads, some four billion salary-earners and their families will be the chief solvent consumers by 2040 — white-collar workers, merchants, doctors, nurses, lawyers, judges, police officers, administrators, teachers, developers, lab research workers, industrial technicians, skilled workers, service employees. Most of them will no longer have a fixed workplace. Accessible at all times, they must permanently monitor their employability, in other words their state of fitness (to perform physical tasks) and their knowledge (for intellectual work). For the youngest, traveling will be a sign of progress toward the hyperclass: the more a sedentary employee travels, the swifter he will climb in his firm's hierarchy.

Just as unskilled manual workers were the dominant social and political force in the first three-quarters of the twentieth century, masses of skilled sedentary workers will dominate the social and political stage over the next three decades.

With the return of nomadism, they will have to suffer. The delocalization of businesses and immigrant workers will push their incomes down. They will miss the days when frontiers were closed and lifetime employment was guaranteed, objects were long-lasting, marriages were sealed and remained sealed, the laws were unbreakable. They will idealize the bureaucrat's status; they will regard guaranteed lifetime employment as an inheritance, and the corresponding salary as a private income. Those who work for what survives of the state or its dependencies will be fewer and fewer, and their status will become more and more precarious. These will use everything to delay the deconstruction of states, including violence.

The middle classes, sedentary by nature, will be fearful of the diseases whose propagation will be accelerated by the nomadic. They will claim the right to grow roots, to work slowly. Some will cloister themselves in the autism of an assiduous use of nomadic objects. They will be narcissistically obsessed by the self-monitors, like the Japanese *otaku*—those fanatics of virtual nomadism, of autistic listening to music, and of the self-monitoring of the body. Others will refuse movement because of obesity: more than a quarter of American adults (31 percent) and a tenth of Europeans are today considered obese. In the long run, more than half of the sedentary population could be affected by this scourge, a reflection of the rejection of the coming nomadism.

For these middle classes, staying insured and entertaining oneself will be the chief response to the world's risks. Insuring oneself will be their obsession, and distracting oneself will be their way of forgetting.

For these billions of sedentaries, insurance industrialists will develop specific products covering the risks of insecurity, joblessness, illness, movement, uncertainty, disorder, in every economic, financial, and cultural field. One day they may even be able to insure themselves against a broken heart, sexual impotence, intellectual shortcomings, or the denial of maternal love.

Entertainment industrialists will invent new ways of letting them share (virtually) the existence of hypernomads and thus allow them access to a *virtual nomadism.*

The middle classes in particular will live the life of the hypernomads by proxy. They will do this by practicing four principal sports, all of them simulating movement, all solitary, all idealized mockups of competition in super-empire, where everyone will be supposed to have a chance. All will be practiced by former elites of previous cores, all will be practicable and will allow progress—horseback riding, golf, sailing, and dance. These travel-simulators will allow them to mime a break with the world while still profiting from its logistics: along secure trails, in domesticated forests, along pirateless shores, with efficient rescue services, clubhouses, havens, and welcoming shelters. To become a good rider, a good golfer, a good sailor or dancer, they will have to display the traveler's qualities (skill, intuition, tolerance, grace, tenacity, courage, clearheadedness, prudence, readiness to share, equilibrium) without having to endure travel's inconveniences. For each of these home sports, self-monitors will allow them to surround themselves with virtual, three-dimensional universes, or else to practice them virtually. These sports will also allow sedentaries to play-act through the demands of competition, to find pleasure in making progress, to familiarize themselves with the self-monitors, to experience the illusion of being hypernomads (although the latter will have abandoned these distractions long since). They will have to give proof of ever stronger emotions.

The sedentaries will also pay increasingly dear to watch (in real time) team sports, themselves sophisticated simulations of hypernomad life. The players in these matches, contested in a spirit of merciless competition, obey increasingly violent, swift, and murderous rules as they try to penetrate the enemy's citadel. This is defended by a sedentary (the goal in soccer) or by other nomads (basketball, American football, rugby, or baseball). These games, the last areas of encounter, will also be the ultimate subjects of conversation. New technologies will make it possible to gain access to them on all media, two- or three-dimensional, and even to use them in order to self-monitor their own emotions. The spectators will be able to join in soccer matches involving thousands of players. The major competitions in these sports (and especially the most popular of them, soccer) will open broad markets for the "business circuses" that manage them.

Still imitating the hypernomads, some of these virtual nomads will also go to swell the ranks of drug consumers: alcohol, cannabis, opium, morphine, heroin, cocaine, synthetic products (amphetamines, methamphetamines, Ecstasy). Chemical, biological, or electronic drugs, distributed by "self-repairers," will become consumer products in a world without law or police, whose chief victims will be the infranomads.

Infranomads: Victims of Super-Empire

Super-empire will in fact raise the market in triumph on a global scale. But it will not bring about the disappearance of poverty, which will afflict a disconcerting share of the planet's population. In 2015, the number of those I call infranomads, who live below the poverty threshold, in other words on less than $1.25 a day, will still be roughly a billion as against 1.4 billion in 2006 and 1.9 billion in 1980. Increasing, yes, but not enough.

Weakened, states will no longer be able to finance decent assistance incomes. Attempts to reduce the number of the poorest through the working of market forces alone will end in failure. Growth will not supply enough jobs; production of specific goods intended for this category will not suffice to give it access to basic goods; on its own, the market will be unable to equip the megalopolises with the infrastructures made necessary by the increased numbers of the citizenry.

From then on, infranomads will be more and more vulnerable to epidemics, to lack of water, to desertification, to climate warming. More and more, they will be forced to move from countryside to cities, then from city to city, to flee indigence and drought, to look for a job and a roof.

They will be increasingly available for every kind of revolt and will feed the pirate economy. They will also be the chief targets for vendors of utopias, and will become the leading players and the first victims of hyperconflict (if it takes place). But they will also be the principal stakes and the great victors of hyperdemocracy (if it ever materializes).

Meanwhile (and this is the worst defeat), no one will be able to organize the governance of super-empire anymore. The market will be a golem without a brain, a plane without a pilot.

The Governance of Super-Empire

This victory of market over democracy will create an utterly novel situation—a market without a state. All the theoreticians recognize that such a market gives rise to the appearance of cartels, underuses productive forces, encourages financial speculation, fosters joblessness, wastes natural resources, liberates the criminal economy, and empowers pirates. Such was the fate in particular of China in 1912, of Somalia in 1990, of Afghanistan in 2002, of Iraq in 2006. Such will be the fate of super-empire.

States, or what remains of them around the year 2050, will no longer be viewed as anything but the successors of businesses. No one will any longer be capable of guaranteeing equality of treatment of citizens, impartial elections, or freedom of information.

The market itself will not be satisfied with this situation. Wherever it has taken up residence, it has always needed a strong state to exist: on the global scale it will need respect for a few rules—so that dishonest players will not distort competition, so that the arms of war do not displace the laws of trading, so that property law is not infringed, so that consumers will remain solvent, and so that violence may be socially mastered.

Insurance and distraction businesses, the market's principal strengths, will try to play these roles. They will produce norms allowing everyone to take his place in the super-empire and offer shows making it possible to escape it. To succeed in this, they will have to lean on specialist, corporate organizations offering a kind of self-proclaimed governance.

Banks and financial institutions will endow themselves (they are already doing so) with global prudential bodies. These organize monthly meetings of the presidents of the world's leading central banks in Basel. This committee has already decreed (under the names "Basel I" and "Basel II") applicable accounting and financial rules (without the prior acquiescence of any global law) to every bank on the planet. Such a coordinating body of all central banks will one day attempt, on its own authority, to fix a stable parity among all the world's major currencies by imposing budgetary norms on states. Then it will create a global quasi-currency in an attempt to counter private currencies.

Other organizations will define rules for checking

on the origins of capital in order to combat the pirate economy. Initially public and later private, these bodies will complete and then replace police action by turning to mercenaries.

Very many other professions (accountants, lawyers, advertising personnel, information specialists, doctors, pharmacists, architects, teachers, engineers), themselves hard-pressed by the insurance companies, will decree norms. They will create specialist organizations, financed by quasi-taxes, to monitor their members and avoid scandals. To do so, they will use all the technologies of hypersurveillance.

Other institutions of governance of the same kind will emerge on the national or continental scale, particularly in the fields of energy, telecommunications, health, and education.

Finally, impartial agencies will establish norms for financial, social, ecological, and ethical orthodoxy. They will influence the behavior of businesses and states—anxious to present a clean image to the markets. In the environmental field in particular, the insurance companies will insist that businesses comply with the norms decreed by such agencies in order to reduce climatic disturbances and the damage caused by natural disasters that might follow in their wake.

"Governance" will thus itself become a particularly profitable sector. Businesses will specialize in it in order to support the insurance companies that gave birth to them. They will little by little take over from national regulators at the planetary level. The ones who carry the day will be those able to acquire private police forces to palliate the weakness of armies and the public police, and to verify application of norms and truthfulness. Governance companies will also appear, supplying businesses with competent members for their administrative boards.

These surveillance organisms will first be dominated by the American empire: ICAAN, which today runs the Internet, constitutes a good example of a self-proclaimed international authority (but in fact a mask for the American government). These organisms will extend American law to the rest of the world before creating their own.

Regulators and insurers will thus be the fragile masters of the governance of super-empire. They will encounter competition and threats, paid for by criminal organizations that will try to eliminate them, as well as threats from other, relational bodies—which they themselves will try to eliminate.

Soccer, which I mentioned above as the planet's leading spectacle, already constitutes a particularly finished example of what will be, tomorrow, this collective governance of super-empire. Indeed, no international body is as powerful in its field as the Fédération Internationale de Football (FIFA), even though the United States plays only a marginal part in it. It already controls the considerable sums the media lavishes on the sport, without any verification of the legitimacy of those who direct it or verification of what it does with these resources. It has its own antidoping labs, which it uses when it chooses. The smallest neighborhood club at the other end of the world feels obliged to respect the tiniest change to the rules emanating from its headquarters in Zurich. The law of nomadic and universal work there is far in advance of national laws.

The same is true for all other federations of major world sports, and even more so for the International Olympic Committee, it too headquartered in Switzerland, in Lausanne.

Like these sports organizations, the other instruments of governance of super-empire will be institutions self-proclaimed for the greater good of their masters. Their doctrine, an apologia for competition, will constitute an idealized representation of super-empire.

These federations will be increasingly controlled by insurance companies that will cover their major risks: thus, in 2003, FIFA took out a specific loan to cover—for up to $262 million—the risk of a cancellation of the 2006 World Cup, threatened notably by terrorist acts. This gave insurance and reinsurance companies effective control of the event.

If these governance institutions should tip over into the criminal economy, they will prepare the moment when (in the second wave of the future) super-empire will be crushed by the pirates. On the other hand, if they manage to inspire general planetary interest, they will contribute to hastening the time when the third wave of the future brings them together in the bosom of a planetary democratic government.

In the Name of Freedom, the End of Freedom

Toward 2050, super-empire will be a world of extreme imbalances and great contradictions. It will fail and collapse, caught up in its own nets. While transparency will make disparities more visible and less tolerable, economic, political, and military cycles will accelerate. Under the pretext of helping men escape scarcity, the market will have to create new forms. Industries will take fewer and fewer risks while demanding (under pressure from the insurers) maximum profitability. Salary-earners will plead in vain that their share of the revenue not shrink. Consumers — and electors to boot — will demand price cuts. With priority going to the short term, to the immediate, to the precarious, and to disloyalty, the task of financing all research and of collecting taxes will become more and more arduous. The insurance companies will be unable to cover all risks. Distraction and information will no longer be able to divert people's attention from the clamor of daily tragedy. Growth, which today gives everyone hope, will no longer serve as an alibi. Hypersurveillance will put a gag on freedom and dry up the wellsprings of innovation.

Nomadism, at the very source of the mercantile order's dynamic, will itself be gradually blocked by the technical limits imposed on travel. Ecological requirements will lead to limitations on airplane flights. Before the end of this century the moon will be colonized; a little later, the interior of the solar system will be colonized. But we shall not be capable of going much farther: at the speed of light, it would take four years and three months to reach the nearest star; and to venture even farther, astronauts would have to live a whole lifetime aboard, gradually replaced by their own children whom they would initiate into the mysteries of space piloting.

The hyperworld of super-empire will not be able to

tolerate being caged within its frontiers. It will not accept the fact that earth is at once the prison and the oasis of humankind. So it will then attempt—it is already doing so—this last astounding feat: exiting from oneself. It is there that man will rediscover his dialogue, endlessly resumed, with his own sexuality. He will try to present himself as an object in order to go and live elsewhere—anywhere that is not himself.

From the very beginning, the human species has sought to distance itself from its own method of reproduction. To differentiate itself from the animal kingdom, it strove first to deny the reproductive function of sexuality, then to give it another meaning. In the ritual order, most cosmogonies insist that not being born of a sexual relation is peculiar to the gods. The monotheistic religions in particular consider sexuality a constraint imposed on men by the forces of evil. The mercantile order, on the contrary, chooses to admit it, while recognizing in it a function different from reproduction—pleasure. Reproduction thus remains (in the mercantile order as in previous orders) an animal constraint that psychiatry (starting at the close of the nineteenth century) aims to make tolerable. In the twentieth century, the mercantile order sought to evacuate the reproductive role of sexuality by making motherhood artificial, by using increasingly sophisticated methods—pills, premature labor, in vitro fertilization, surrogate mothers. In super-empire, the mercantile order will even go so far as to dissociate reproduction and sexuality. Sexuality will be the kingdom of pleasure, reproduction that of machines.

Hypersurveillance, self-surveillance, and then self-repair will provide what is needed for it. After repairing diseased organs they will want to produce them, then create replacement bodies. First they will produce lineages of stem cells without destroying the embryo, which will make genetic therapy ethically acceptable, and then reproductive cloning. Finally, they will manufacture the human being like a made-to-measure artifact, in an artificial uterus, which will allow the brain to further develop with characteristics chosen in advance. The human being will thus have become a commercial object.

Thanks to the astounding progress we can expect from the nanosciences, everyone will even hope to transfer his awareness of himself to another body, to acquire his own double, copies of beloved people, dream men and women, hybrids built with peculiar traits preselected to reach precise objectives. Some will even seek to overtake the human species with a life-form endowed with a different and superior intelligence.

In this ultimate vision of super-empire, death will be delayed until the disappearance of the last clone possessing consciousness of himself, even until all clones born of himself by all the other clones born of others are forgotten.

Then man, at last manufactured like an artifact, will no longer know death. Like all industrial objects, he will no longer be able to die, since he will never have been born.

But well before humankind transforms itself into machines, well before super-empire takes command, man will have succeeded in resisting this prospect — he is already resisting it. Super-empire will collapse. It will be smashed to pieces on the shore. Men will throw everything into the fight to avoid such a nightmare.

After the violence of money will come (is already coming) the violence of arms.

5

Second Wave of the Future: Planetary War

The disappearance of the Soviet system and the spread of democracy seem to have made war a remote prospect. The arms race is over. All countries seem to have realized that economic growth brought them much more than conquest. Never, in fact, has the world as a whole been so pacific, in appearance at least. There is today no war between two countries for the first time in more than six decades.

And yet, as with the ending of every form, at the same time as states are unmaking themselves and super-empire looms on the horizon, a new pre-war begins. When the market is universal, differences are flattened out and each entity becomes everyone's rival. When the state weakens, the possibility of channeling and mastering violence disappears. Local conflicts multiply, identities are threatened, ambitions clash, human lives no longer have value. The disappearance of the Soviet Union has eliminated one of the world's policemen. And further, the coming failure of super-empire, the sophistication of weaponry, and the proliferation of players might even converge (in the bosom of super-empire) to trigger a global conflict. It will be a planetary conflagration, a hyperconflict far more destructive than all previous wars, local or global. Here is the story of its possible beginnings.

Regional Ambitions

Between now and 2025, with the step-by-step advent of a polycentric order, new regional powers will burst forth, all of them wanting access to the same riches. They will create the military means to match their ambitions. Among them will be all the powers that dominate this period and a few others, more marginal, more bellicose.

Fascinated by the way in which empires are born and die, China (whose military spending, even today, is particularly low) will seek to become a major power once again, including on the strategic plane. One way or another, it will seek to take back Taiwan and consolidate its hegemony over East Asia, as the United States did over the Americas in the nineteenth century. It will lean on South Korea, forcing it to arm. It will let North Korea's totalitarian regime linger on; that country too will seek to acquire new means (which will include the nuclear) of defending itself. Japan in turn will rearm in order to resist a Korean threat and the increasing power of China. India will refuse to have itself encircled by Muslim powers. Even if it does not become an Islamic state, Pakistan will seek to defend itself against India and ensure its ascendancy over its neighbors, from Afghanistan to Kashmir. Indonesia will try to equip itself with the means of ensuring the direction of Islam as a whole and of dominating Southeast Asia. Australia itself will want to affirm its influence over the region and protect itself against Indonesia's designs.

Shiite Iran will try to control Islam, to the great detriment of the chiefly Arab Sunnis. To achieve this, the former Persia will have at its disposal a vast population, a lot of money and petroleum, and a geostrategic position. Turkey will refuse to abandon control of the Turkish-speaking world to Iran. Saudi Arabia, the unpredictable vassal of the United States, will try to remain a dominating player in its own region. Egypt will have every reason to see itself as the biggest potential power in the Arab world. Israel will try to remain a regional power in order to survive. Algeria and Morocco will quarrel for preeminence in the Maghreb. Despite threats of disarticulation, Nigeria and Congo, whose birth rates are soaring, will want to control the regions around them. South Africa will want to dominate its neighbors to ensure that it does not remain locked into its enclave.

Russia will attempt to recover its global status and will consider itself in the front line against Islam and China. To defend itself against these neighbors, it will rearm and weave a web of military alliances stretching along its pipeline system. In Western Europe, Germany and France might each rediscover a regional ambition, if the European Union can no longer channel their rivalry.

Brazil will seek to dominate the southern hemisphere of the Americas. Venezuela will strive to challenge it for this role and gather around it the Andean countries, with a view to expelling the United States from the region. Mexico and Argentina will refuse to be marginalized. In Mexico in particular, major political and social revolts will endanger its alliance with the United States, while Canada will seek to remain neutral. The demands of the war on drug dealers, imposed by the United States, will also require a major reinforcement of Mexico's military potential.

All these regional ambitions will clash. We shall see a Latin America in revolt against the American economic and political presence, an Arab world dreaming of eliminating Israel, a coalition of Persians seeking to upset the Arab world, a Russia wanting to dominate part of Europe all over again and at the same time protect itself against China and Islam. India and Pakistan will attempt to remove one another from areas that border them; China and Russia will covet the same border regions. Japan, the United States, and China will fight for domination over East Asia.

Military alliances will form, sometimes associating improbable partners. Iran will cooperate with China and Russia; China with Pakistan; Russia with the European Union; Pakistan, Egypt, Indonesia, and Iran could unite in a Muslim confederation. The small countries of Southeast Asia, now members of ASEAN, will unite militarily to escape American, Chinese, or Japanese domination; Iran and Venezuela will seek support from Russia and China; the European Union will seek closer ties with the United States; Russia will seek ties with Algeria and already sends arms to Venezuela, which has requested observer status in . . . the Arab League!

These clashing ambitions, first on diplomatic and economic terrain, may lead to military confrontations between states. Very venerable forces — pirates and mercenaries — will enter the lists.

Pirate Armies, Corsair Armies

In matters of global violence, states have never been the sole players. Mafias, gangs, terrorist movements — I call them pirates here — have always intervened between nations to fight them or, at the very least, to violate their laws. When deconstruction weakens states, and law and the police become more discrete, violence will spread in public life and between individuals. These pirates will even become essential agents of the economy and of geopolitics.

As soon as the ninth form reaches its limits and super-empire begins, pirates will be more numerous and more powerful than ever. They will no longer seek to make a nest in the bosom of super-empire; they will no longer be satisfied to profit from a cold war. Whether their motives are criminal or political, they will have neither territories nor even families to protect and will be free to consolidate their power over the world. The more super-empire develops, the more powerful they will be, without a state police with the means to fight them.

These pirates will be of several kinds.

Some nations that unmake themselves under the pressures of the market and the workings of democracy will give birth to pirate entities, blurred zones without law, pirate states or nonstates. They will be in the hands of war leaders at the head of overarmed groups controlling regions, ports, pipelines, roads, and raw materials. This is already the case with Somalia, with Transnistria (on the Moldovan-Ukrainian border), part of Ethiopia, Sri Lanka, Afghanistan, Pakistan, among many other regions of Africa and Asia.

As we have seen, cities that have grown too fast will also become pirate kingdoms in which no army and no police will ever dare venture. This is already the case (among others) with certain conglomerations in Brazil, Nigeria, Congo, and Colombia. They too will equip themselves with increasingly sophisticated arms.

Mafia-style organizations, cartels, white-collar criminals, and leading drug traffickers will operate without a geographical base. They will collect funds, issuing threats and behaving like states—and against states—in order to guarantee their security. They will equip themselves (they are already equipping themselves) with the most sophisticated arms. They will threaten judges, police, and political leaders likely to put themselves in their path. Sometimes, as is already the case in Colombia, Somalia, Brazil, and Pakistan, these bands will control cities, territories, even whole countries. Hypernomads (chemists, intellectuals, accountants, engineers, military officers, financiers) will put themselves at their service and take part alongside them.

Political or religious groups, they too without a territorial base, will acquire all possible military means to take control of a country, expel its occupants, and then destroy the mercantile order. This is the case, for example, with al-Qaeda and other nihilist movements within its sphere.

Other pirate forms will be born. The proliferation of violence and rage, provoked by the advent of super-empire, will lead to outrages of a new kind. Masses of infranomads, with nothing in common but traveling together, could become threatening. Just like the nomadic masses that crossed the Rhine in the year 406, hordes with weapons in their hands could cross the Strait of Gibraltar, the river Amur, or the Usumacinta waterway — menacing, no longer begging.

Some of these forces could form a league against states, and in particular against democracies. We shall see (we are already seeing) drug barons in the service of political causes or using immigrants as ferrymen or smugglers. We shall see (we are already seeing) nations in ruins become mafia lairs. We shall see (we are already seeing) terrorist forces — by nature nomadic — finding refuge in nonstates. We shall see (we are already seeing) Mafia-style organizations supporting political, secular, or religious opinions, as the Mafia itself once did, or French gangsters who turned collaborationist in 1940. We shall see (we are already seeing) acts of urban violence so extreme that they will require responses more military than police in nature.

Confronted with these threats or acts of aggression, nations will need increasing numbers of soldiers and policemen capable of risking their lives. But fewer and fewer volunteers will come forward, and public opinion in market democracies will no longer want deaths in their armies, and still less among conscripts. Already today, only one-half of one percent of the American population is under arms, and every soldier killed is a national tragedy. To carry out the missions it has taken on, the American empire—like the Roman Empire of yore—will have to incorporate more and more foreigners into its own forces. Two percent of the American armed forces—some 300,000—are already made up of immigrants not yet naturalized. Their numbers are increasing substantially since the decree of July 4, 2002, which speeds up the naturalization of foreigners joining the army (an almost identical copy of a decree by the emperor Hadrian, which goes back to the year 138 of our era . . .).

Nor will this suffice. Corsairs will have to stand up to the pirates. Mercenary businesses will develop, employing former military men. They will be used as suppliers of men to armies and police. In Africa there are a hundred companies of this kind, supplying men and matériel to governments, businesses, even to international organizations. They will soon be exercising general security functions: defense, protection, even attack. Industrial businesses will legally finance such mercenaries, whom they will place at the service of governments from whom they seek markets. Some of these mercenary companies will be used to restore peace in places where the intervention forces of the United Nations or the Organization of African Unity (OAU) have failed, as was already the case with Sierra Leone. The UN will even have its own offices protected by mercenaries. Some countries will use them more or less openly to wage war at a distance against every kind of trafficker, without visibly committing their own forces. Among these mercenary companies, some will obey a good-conduct code obliging them to respect the laws of war, while others will adhere to the Geneva Conventions. Most of them — like the governments they serve — will no longer respect any constraint. The practice of torture in Iraq and the fate reserved for the prisoners at Guantánamo are premonitory signs of this trend.

The Anger of the Secular

Then the anger of peoples will erupt against the mercantile order and above all against the United States, which will direct it for another twenty years at least. A secular anger, based on rational premises.

Hatred against a core is not unleashed when the core is at the peak of its power, but when it begins to decline. This was the fate of all the previous cores: it will be the fate of the American empire. Triumphant at the falling of the Berlin Wall, Washington has already become the chief target of a wave of criticism challenging globalization and market democracy.

Now a critical coalition will emerge, targeting America and the mercantile order. It will embrace all those who expect nothing more from them or who are frustrated at not receiving their benefits. They will criticize America pell-mell, along with the West, globalization, market democracy, and the coming super-empire. Antiglobalists of every hue, most will have nothing to propose in their place.

Their criticism will first be directed (is already being directed) at the invasive role of the United States, which monopolizes the essentials of the world's wealth, wastes its resources, disturbs its climate, enslaves peoples, claims the right to rule them as it pleases, and violates many rules of the democracy it aspires to dictate to others.

Next, the criticism will focus on the markets. This will be all the easier as the facts establish more and more clearly that markets suppress neither poverty nor joblessness nor exploitation; that they concentrate all powers in a few hands, inflicting insecurity on increasingly numerous majorities; that they shelve long-term requirements; that they compete with one another to destabilize the climate; that they create scarcities and invent new cost-free arrangements in order to profit from them later. They will protest that hope and the quality of life are not at all the same from one place to another in the world; that the targets of their anger will become —with hypersurveillance and self-surveillance—one of the most pernicious and absolute forms of dictatorship. And finally, the markets will be reproached for liberating violence by orienting all desires toward a hungering for mercantile objects, including a hunger for arms.

It will then also be easy to denounce democracy as an illusion, in which the wealthiest concentrate in their hands the powers of informing, distracting, knowing, monitoring, healing, teaching, channeling, deciding, and accumulating. These new ideologues will explain that parliamentary democracy, like the market, is a deception, the instrument of armed forces and big businesses; that it generates disparities, destroys nature, and undermines moral values. They will even argue that it is but a convenient excuse invoked by Americans to hold on to their power without losing their souls—while they shut their eyes on the development of the pirate economy wherever it is useful to them.

The mercantile order will thus be justly accused of being for many (and by its very nature) a source of wretchedness, injustice, insecurity, disorder, waste, ecological upheavals, immorality, identity destruction, violation of religious rules, and oppression. Many will also denounce with a single voice both market and democracy as machines for manufacturing disloyalty, for annihilating all forms of morality and social organization, and for destroying the freedom they claim to promote. They will complain of having to go and live wherever the market needs their labor, of having to leave the places where their roots were once deep, and of lacking the financial means to acquire the promised freedom. They will rail at no longer being able to influence the world through their vote, of being dominated, monitored, self-monitored, self-produced, and of being forced to comply with norms fixed by the demands of profit.

Others will go so far as to condemn the very principle of an individual freedom that leads to being loyal only to oneself, to no longer feeling bound by an oath or a contract. They will complain that they are constantly required to auction off their obligations, their feelings, their values, their faith, and the fate of their children, always ready to abandon, and at all moments expecting to be abandoned, without the needs of future generations ever being taken into account. Apologia for dictatorship will once again become a respectable subject of conversation.

And finally, many will profit from the progressive weakening of states to let their impulses toward violence develop, freed of all constraint. The first freedom will be freedom to kill, gratuitously and without goal or strategy.

The cities (where every form of alienation will abound, along with all the proofs that market democracy is only — for the overriding majority of humans — a gigantic moral swindle) will become the principal nests of revolt. They will harbor more and more serial criminals, they will breed an infinity of killings.

Unlike the Communist revolutionaries of the past, whose aim was to build another society in place of capitalism, most of these new contestants will propose no system of substitution. Ever since communism failed, no utopia has seemed available either to replace the market or to replace democracy. Except for a handful who will propose a return to theocracy.

The Anger of Believers

If, according to the Judeo-Greek ideal, the mercantile order represents the welcome and successful outcome of progress and individuality, it also constitutes the worst enemy for religious believers — because in it, human freedom comes before God's commands, and particularly because it endangers the stability of the family on which transmission of faith depends. These believers will make the secular criticism directed at the market and democracy their own.

The two great evangelizing religions, Christianity

and Islam, will be in the thick of this battle. Each in its own way will co-opt the secular arguments, and even find justification for conflict and violence among themselves and against the mercantile order.

Some Christian movements will reproach (they are already reproaching) the market and democracy with secreting frivolous desires, with looking kindly on lechery and infidelity. They will accuse them of commercializing moral values, of letting science think the world differently from what the letter of the holy texts prescribes, of no longer giving a meaning to death, of decreeing a law different from that of the Bible. They will in particular oppose all forms of abortion, of birth control, of euthanasia. They will express regret that materialist concerns distance men from any kind of self-questioning about the Beyond. Some will proclaim the supremacy of Christian values over the laws of men, and even over reason. Some of them will go so far as to consider that the use of force is theologically permitted.

The Catholic Church, the first nomadic, "stateless," and borderless empire, long used force to oppose reason, science, progress, the mercantile order, the rights of capitalists and those of entrepreneurs and workers — before resigning itself to them. Some of its members will again become increasingly radical, closer to its initial ideals. With increasing vehemence, some Catholics will reproach liberalism with denying the divine order. They will launch more and more attacks on democracy, the market, and Judeo-Greek ideals in order to stand in uncompromising defense of the purity of the faith. Others in the church will continue to stand up for nonviolence, love, and justice.

Protestant churches will be in the vanguard of these struggles, especially the evangelicals. Originating in several southern U.S. states — the Bible Belt — they muster seventy million American citizens, who include several hundred thousand propagandizing ministers. Evangelism already rules over certain departments of many American universities, where it censors teaching of the sciences and other religions. These churches will be more and more influential politically. They will be behind more and more decisions by Congress and the American state apparatus. The speeches and actions of the previous American president were increasingly influenced by them. To hear them, via a slow semantic shift, it will no longer be the values of democracy that the West must defend but those of Christianity. These churches will urge women to return to the home and produce more and more children.

At the moment when the emergence of super-empire seriously threatens the very existence of the United States, some of these churches might go so far as to encourage America to wage war against Islam, and even against democracy and capitalism. The only one among the major democracies not to have known dictatorship, the United States could then (around 2040) fall prey to a theocratic temptation, explicit or implicit, in the shape of a *theocratic isolationism* in which democracy would be no more than a shadowy presence.

In Africa and Latin America the citizenry, whose destitution can only get worse, will be increasingly attuned to the discourse of these evangelical churches, which by now are major financial, ideological, military, and political powers. More than twenty-five million people in Brazil are already followers of evangelism. They are present in Japan, China, India, and Indonesia. They could well form alliances here and there with secular pirates and traffickers in arms, women, and drugs. They will also stand face to face against Islam — and the struggle will be relentless. They will defend Christians in countries where they are in a minority, as in Lebanon, Syria, Iraq, and Palestine. They will even attempt, with a certain success, to convert Muslims — Kurdish minorities in Iraq and Syria, Berbers in the Maghreb — by offering them social assistance and promising them visas for the United States and Europe as "persecuted Christians."

In Europe, we shall also see Christian churches speaking out explicitly against capitalism. We shall hear the faithful, Catholic parties, and religious authorities denouncing the burden of the market, freedom of movement, and its institutional translation: the European Union. Religious values will recover political visibility. Already, among European political figures, no one until very recently would have dared frame the problem of Turkey's adhesion to the European Union in religious terms. Nor would they have made the theological question a key dimension of the European constitutional debate. Far-right parties will draw increasingly on these religious values to defend their own programs. They too will explicitly urge women to return to the home and raise children. Several European democracies might one day enshrine Christianity in their constitutions, and even openly become theocracies. The Vatican will play a central part in this evolution. It could choose to forge alliances with the other monotheisms or, to the contrary, urge war against them, and in particular against Islam.

Within Islam as well, very diverse forces will increasingly bring democracy, market, globalization, the United States, Israel, Europe, Judaism, and Christianity under their critical lash. If nothing is done, a major divorce will take place between a part of Islam and the West.

In 2008, 1.3 billion human beings were Muslims; in other words, a third fewer than Christians. Although Islam in itself is no more intolerant than the other monotheisms, and although it was Islam that brought Judeo-Greek thought to Europe, the countries where it dominates today are all theocracies or secular dictatorships, with the exception of a handful that are democracies-in-progress: Turkey, Algeria, Morocco, Kuwait, Senegal. In all the others, it is almost impossible to build churches or synagogues, to convert to another religion, to live as an atheist, or to marry a non-Muslim unless he or she converts. The dominant ideology consists of believing that any answer to any question is in the Koran, that every intellectual is useless, and that the origin of every problem (from AIDS to poverty) is the work of the "infidels." Economically, socially, and culturally, these countries are among the world's least developed (in all the Muslim countries, there are fewer translations of foreign books than in Greece alone), even though the vagaries of distribution of natural resources make some Muslims the wealthiest people in the world.

At the moment, there are few voices within Islam to demand its compliance with human rights laws. Doubtless one day, under the combined pressure of economic growth and the demands of youth and of women, theologians will lead it along the road to tolerance and democracy. They insist on surats dating from before 622 rather than those that follow, and they are rediscovering the philosophy of Ibn Rushd (better known in the West as Averroes). Meanwhile certain minority elements within Islam (Christianity's leading adversary and similarly evangelical) yearn to recover its eleventh-century glory, to gather together from Córdoba to Baghdad, then spread across the whole planet — demographically, through conversion, and even, for some, through war.

Besides, the dominant face of Islam is not the believer but the pilgrim, the preacher, the converted, the proselyte. In principle, conversion is individual and without political connotations. It must be carried out in the name of an ideal of purity, of solidarity, of submission to male power. Muslims are forbidden to change religion in general on pain of death. In practice, conversion is (and will continue to be) political. Islam will strive to gather in those who everywhere criticize the mercantile order, and to convert numbers of the secular emerging from what I earlier called the "critical coalition."

By promising fellowship in a community (the *Umma*), Islam will elicit more and more echoes among the isolated, the weak, the vanquished, the rebellious. It will launch social programs among the critically destitute, promising them what the market does not offer — concrete forms of solidarity, charity, and dignity, allowing them to escape solitude and hope for paradise.

Its capacity to convert is not yet great. In France,

for example, only thirty-six hundred people a year convert to Islam, and in 2008 total converts numbered seventy thousand. That rate is unlikely to rise.

It is demography that will be the main factor in Muslim population growth. There will be more than 1.8 billion Muslims in 2020 (a quarter of the world's population), and they will probably have surpassed the number of Christians. Their expansion will slow as economic growth slows their birth rate, one of the highest in the world.

The most intransigent thinkers in Islam will demand that the faithful, wherever they might be, should obey no laws other than those of God, and reject any secular constitution. All begins with Ibn Hanbal (780–855) and Ibn Taymiyya, who died in 1328, and who attempted to impose literal obedience to the text of the Koran. Then came Abdel Wahhab (1703–1792), still very influential today, who insisted that a Muslim must obey no other law than that of the Koran, rejected the intercession of saints and excommunicated (*takfir*) liberals, thus ushering in the peak of the *salafiyya* (the path of the ancestors). Along the same lines, some today follow the Pakistani theologian Sayyid Mawdudi (1903–1979), who opposed the creation of a secular Pakistani state during the partition of India. He also forbade allegiance to any other legislation than that of the Koran. For all of them, the only sovereignty is the exclusive political sovereignty of God alone. Mawdudi presented Islam as the third way between capitalism and socialism, and wished to make a theocratic state of united Islam.

So that Islamic law should thus be rigorously respected and not challenged by its confrontation with different value systems, increasingly numerous voices will call for the constitution of a theocratic Muslim empire— which for some of them will come about through war.

For others, this empire must first of all rebuild itself in the lands of past glory, stretching from Córdoba to Baghdad. Some twenty years ago Sayyid Qutb, leader of the Muslim Brotherhood and a disciple of Mawdudi, called for an Islamic revolution allowing the passage from the Jahiliyya, the ante-Islamic period, to the Hakimiyya, the sovereignty of God ("total rebellion in every place on earth, expulsion of the usurpers of divine sovereignty who direct men according to laws emanating from themselves"). For him, we must translate surat XII.40, which reads "the *hukum* belongs to God alone," as "supreme power belongs to God alone," not by the classic "judgment belongs to God alone." In other words, a theocracy instead of an individual moral relationship with God. The thrust of his project was the fusion of the Umma islamiyya (the best of the communities to have emerged for men) and the Dar al-Islam, the kingdom ruled by Islamic law. Qutb, whose disciples are still countless, wished to fight against every Muslim not faithful to his vision of Islam, and against every "infidel." Among many others today, the London-based Hizb ul Tahrir (Liberation Party) also calls for the rebirth of this "caliphate" by war (*harb*).

In Shiite Islam, the Ayatollah Khomeini sought from the early sixties to impose the idea of war as a tool of conversion, and hailed martyrdom, suicide, and the *chadid*. "The sword," he wrote, "is the key to Paradise."

For others still, war must target the whole world. The empire of Islam must spread all over the planet, without a center or a dominant nation, to make of it a kind of theological empire.

Supporters of this Islamic war for reconquest of the Caliphate and conquest of the world today define a three-stage military strategy: "In territories where it is still in a minority, Islam must practice 'provisional peace,' which can be denounced at any moment.

"In territories where it will have converted or expelled a significant fraction of the population, it must install a Dar al-Harb, or 'war zone.' The last believers in other monotheisms will provisionally be tolerated there, with an inferior status—that of *dhimmi* ('protected'). Believers in other philosophies and atheists will be expelled.

"In territories where Muslim power will have become totally dominant, all believers in another monotheism must be converted or expelled: the Jews, because they did not accept the Koran in Medina; the Christians, because they place Jesus above Muhammad. All 'infidels' there will be declared enemies, because 'unbelief is a single nation.'"

Some groups adopting this strategy—as al-Qaeda did when it was created in 1996—will first of all seek to drive Christian troops from the vicinity of Mecca, where they have been stationed since 1991—even if they have to fight Arab regimes to do it. The *fitna* ("discord") between Muslims will thus be salutary for them. Next they will want to eliminate Christians and Jews from the Holy Places of Iraq and Jerusalem, then take power in Lebanon, in Egypt, in North Africa, in Central Asia, in Indonesia, and Pakistan. After that, they will seek to expel all believers in Judeo-Greek philosophy from lands earlier conquered in part by Islam, ranging from Spain to China.

Other groups, like al-Qaeda today, will advocate (even before attempting to restore Muslim Europe) an immediate holy war against the American empire, Israel, Europe, the market, and democracy. Like late-nineteenth-century nihilists, they will seek only to destroy, without the aim (even utopian) of substituting another society for the one they condemn. Besides, al-Qaeda will soon be but one movement among others, the inspirer of countless tiny groups arising from local initiatives.

Other belief systems (and these are the most numerous) will put Islam at the service of nationalist claims, as Islam's ideologues have always ended by doing. This embraces the twelfth-century Almohades, all the way down to the eighteenth century, then Turkey's Rafah movement, Algeria's Front Islamique de Salut (FIS), Palestinian Hamas, Egypt's Muslim Brotherhood, and Lebanon's Hezbollah.

The Asian world, which will soon contain a majority of the world's population, will itself be concerned by these challenges. Although no one wages war in the name of Buddhism, Confucianism, or Hinduism, Islam will try to gain absolute power in every Asian country where it is already dominant, from Pakistan to Indonesia. In those countries very numerous extremist religious schools are to be found.

Moreover, a number of national cultures will use the religious weapon to defend themselves (like the Tibetans) and to regain a lost national identity.

Finally, diverse sects of variegated origins, like those of Moon in Korea, Falun Gong in China, and the

Church of Scientology in the United States, will develop thanks to the spiritual and moral void create by superempire. There are already more members of Falun Gong (whose leader, Li Hongzhi, is reputed to have saved twenty-four worlds . . .) than members of the Chinese Communist Party! And some of these sects will also forge alliances with very questionable partners to hurl themselves into the melee, armed to the teeth.

The Weapons of Hyperconflict

In all ages, the outcome of wars has been decided by possession of new arms and by the price attached by each belligerent to the lives of its own soldiers. In their time, the archers at the battle of Crécy, the tanks of the First World War, and the atomic weapons of the Second World War decided the fate of battles.

In all ages, new weapons have appeared, at once the products and the midwives of civilian technologies: the propeller was born with the lever, firearms with mechanization, tanks with the automobile. Inversely, it was in the armed forces that the telegraph, the radio, energy, the nuclear weapon, and the Internet were born alongside many other technological innovations.

In the next fifty years, new technologies will be developed by armies before being used on the civilian market. For defense or police needs, governments will finance the research needed for perfection of the technologies of hypersurveillance and self-surveillance. Inversely, these technologies will then have civil applications.

In fact, these future weapons will essentially be founded on the concept of surveillance. Armies will at once develop digital infrastructures of nomadic ubiquity, surveillance systems for suspect movements, the means of protecting strategic installations, and a network of economic intelligence. Robots (concealed in enemy territory) and drones (flying robots) will relay data, detect chemical or biological agents, and serve as scouts ahead of infantry detachments faced with mined areas or blind spots. Software simulating battle will be permanently updated as close as possible to the battlefields.

Furthermore, new combat units will be integrated with the means of simulation, surveillance, and striking. New networks and instruments of nomadic ubiquity will allow combatants to stay connected and simulate every kind of situation. Intelligent clothing will serve to manufacture new uniforms; new materials will make it possible to design new shields. Three-dimensional simulation technologies will help prepare and carry out combat missions, while robots will work as substitutes for real fighters. Electronic systems (e-bombs) will be able to destroy communications grids and leave an opposing force blind and deaf.

Marines will play a new part in the fight against traffickers, in emigration surveillance, and in the protection of strategic straits. Fighter aircraft will no longer be as useful as today, and will lose their influence over staff thinking and military budgets.

New, so-called conventional weapons will be all the more necessary as unconventional weapons (nuclear and other) become more and more widely disseminated.

The five great powers authorized by treaty to

possess nuclear arms will deploy for a long time to come more than five thousand nuclear warheads, most of them aboard submarines and launched by ultra-precise ballistic missiles. Among these five powers, some will reserve for themselves the possibility of using tactical nuclear weapons—in other words short-range weapons destined for operational use and no longer as instruments of deterrence. These could even be miniaturized to the point where they would be usable by a single combatant, as was already the case during the cold war. India, Israel, and Pakistan, nuclear powers for the past thirty years, will also equip themselves with nuclear submarines able to launch nuclear-capable ballistic missiles designed to reach any potentially hostile or rival capital. North Korea, too, which launched its first nuclear-weapon test in the mid-2000s, will acquire ballistic missiles with a range of about five thousand miles, its declared motive being to forearm itself against any attempt to destabilize its regime. Faced with this threat, Japan will not hesitate much longer to equip itself with arms of the same type to counter the weapons Pyongyang's leaders might launch against it. Four months will suffice, from the moment the decision is taken, for it to acquire the weapon. Iran, obviously, will do the same or come very close to it—unless a clash (which we shall later discuss) takes place. Others will follow along the same path. First it will be Egypt and Turkey, then (probably) Indonesia, Australia, Brazil, and Saudi Arabia. By 2040 or 2050, a total of more than fifteen countries will openly possess nuclear weapons and the means to deliver them.

Shortage of oil will also impel the most diverse

countries toward the production of civil nuclear power stations. This will lead them to use recycled wastes, known as MOX, for fuel — further multiplying the risks of proliferation and also of "disappearance" of wastes (during the transfer of these radioactive materials). Such wastes could then be used to manufacture radiological weapons mingling nuclear wastes and conventional explosives.

Other weapons — chemical, biological, bacteriological, electronic, and nanotechnological — will then appear. As with the new civil technologies they will prefigure, scientists will strive to increase their power, their miniaturization, and their accuracy. Chemical arms will be capable of seeking out and killing leaders without being detected; pandemics could be ready for unleashing at will; complex genetic arms may one day be directed specifically against certain ethnic groups. Nanorobots as small as a mote of dust, known as gray jelly, could carry out stealth surveillance missions and attack the cells of enemy bodies. Then, once animal cloning techniques have progressed, cloned animals could well carry out missions — living animal bombs, monsters out of nightmare.

These weapons will not be developed solely in the military laboratories of powerful countries but also by big businesses, "circus businesses," which will find new markets for them. As always, armaments will remain at the heart of the industrial apparatus, and until superempire is here, public markets will be essentially oriented toward the armaments sector. Big insurance firms and mercenary companies will then pick up the torch.

Most of these weapons will be accessible to small

nations, to nonstates, to corsairs, to pirates, mercenaries, maquisards, mafias, terrorists, and every kind of trafficker. In the not distant future, for example, it will be possible to make an e-bomb for $400 from a condenser, a reel of copper wire, and an explosive. Chemical, radiological, and biological weapons will thus be affordable to everyone. Killing more and more people with rudimentary means will become a sad possibility. In cities and on mass transport, crowding will multiply the effectiveness of the most primitive weapons.

Finally (and perhaps especially), since no war can be won unless the peoples waging it believe it just and necessary, and unless the loyalty of citizens and their belief in its values are maintained, the chief weapons of the future will be the instruments of propaganda, communication, and intimidation.

Arming, Forging Alliances

Confronted with these multiform threats, directed chiefly against them, the market democracies (particularly the masters of the polycentric order) will realize that they can no longer react effectively in dispersed order. They will realize too that defense budgets would be better used if their equipment were technically and mutually compatible, and placed under coordinated command.

The United States will continue to modernize all its weapons systems — conventional, electronic, nuclear, chemical, and bacteriological. A new unit of the U.S. Army, the Future Combat Systems, will soon be composed of highly mobile ground troops, equipped with high-precision conventional weapons, a communications grid, the means of dissimulation, and robots and air units—with or without pilots. This unit could be deployed anywhere in the world within four days. The delay between detection of a target and its destruction will thus be close to zero, whereas it was three days during the Gulf War and five minutes in Iraq. Such a system will be meaningless unless the United States, using a satellite network, equips itself with a digital planetary infrastructure.

The cost of these new weapons will be enormous, with the United States expending $500 billion on them. A million American soldiers will remain temporarily deployed on four continents, supported by thousands of aircraft and ships, before withdrawing to the exclusive defense of American national territory. For the next forty years, defense will continue to represent more than a quarter of the American federal budget—sometimes with enormous wastage caused by the need to create jobs in every electoral constituency for the congressmen whose voice will be essential during the vote on the defense budget.

The Europeans—who together spend five times less on their defense than the United States today—will themselves, after much criticism of American belligerence, be forced to find ways of financing digital infrastructures and the new weapons systems. To do this, they will create increasingly overlapping armed forces and police, harmonize their equipment, and coordinate with the United States, if only for communications and data exchange.

China and India will also increase their military

budgets (now fifteen times lower than that of the United States) to reach at least French or British levels. They will acquire the same weapons, most of them home-manufactured. Japan and Russia will do the same.

To share these mushrooming costs, several of these nations will pool a part of their units in a military force serving the international community and mingling conventional troops with police forces. They will thus form (at first occasionally, then institutionally) an alliance against pirates and enemies of the mercantile order. NATO, founded to counter the Soviet threat, will perhaps become the foundation of this unified force, which will sometimes also serve as part of the United Nations armed forces. In certain cases, India, China, and several of the Eleven will join them.

The Alliance will one day expand to include the biggest firms of super-empire, particularly the military ones. It will then incorporate national armies and privately owned mercenary forces under one flag.

All members of the Alliance will be concerned to monitor "the friends of our enemies." The Muslims of Europe, America, or China, for example, may one day be required to supply proof that they are unconnected with this or that hostile entity, as the Japanese had to do in the 1940s or the Communists in the 1950s. Similarly, if Mexico one day comes to be considered by the United States as a dangerously revolutionary country, the increasingly numerous Latinos will be subject to strict surveillance.

Around 2035 or 2040, the Alliance will realize that it lacks the means to maintain its domination of the mercantile order. Financially and morally exhausted by these conflicts, faced with the same dilemmas as the Roman Empire at the beginning of our era, member countries will then form the polycentric order and change strategy. The Alliance will no longer concern itself with the rest of the world. It will reduce its energy and financial dependence, inaugurate a policy of protectionism, circle its wagons, and limit its defense to the protection of its interests in the narrowest sense. It will try to put in place a shield over its territory to monitor and destroy any weapon or hijacked aircraft attempting to touch its soil. Higher and higher walls will be built against pirates, just like the wall now protecting and isolating Israel from terrorist attacks. For example, the Alliance will deem it essential to master the situation in the western and eastern Mediterranean, usually at the request of the countries concerned. To fly to the countries of the Alliance, people will have to supply detailed information on their lives — and perhaps leave possessions or loved ones behind as security, or as hostages.

Here again, and once again, cutting-edge technologies of market democracy — those of hypersurveillance — will participate in setting up the sinews of war and the police.

Even so, there will be no guarantee of success. Neither markets nor democracies nor pirates can be kept down forever.

Negotiating, Assisting

Some, in Europe or elsewhere, will then propose ceasing to defend themselves, reducing military budgets, disarming unilaterally, and collaborating with whoever is the enemy. We shall witness the birth of these denuclearized, pacifist, and passive postnational states, already the dream of the German philosopher Jürgen Habermas, among many others.

Others, anxious to keep the peace without submitting, will try to give proof of diplomatic imagination. The United Nations will attempt to implement the procedures enshrined in its charter for negotiation, conflict prevention, and dissuasion. So that questions in litigation may be treated in a more confidential way, discreet conflict-prevention bodies will multiply, on the lines of the Organization for Security and Cooperation in Europe (OSCE) or the Community of Sant'Egidio, a discreet and efficient Catholic organization. The latter is connected to the Carter Center, where the former U.S. president has run it remarkably well for over twenty years. A more recent initiative still is that of another former president, Bill Clinton. The role of these ad hoc institutions and specialist relational enterprises will be to detect in advance the sources of conflict and areas of tension, to try to broker agreements between the potential belligerents and ensure they are respected. To do this, they will have to benefit from considerable observation, surveillance, analysis, and prevention capabilities. They must also have enough influence for the agreements reached under their guidance to be respected. We shall encounter them again, in the following wave of the future, as an essential factor for peace.

To avoid war, the market democracies will also try to extend the blessings of freedom to those who might become their enemies. They will help still uncertain countries to join their ranks, in other words to set up the separation of religious and secular powers, to rid themselves of terrorist militias, and lay the foundations for a market economy. Such goals are generally illusory, as is borne out by what is happening in Afghanistan today (a narco-state where the drug trade represents nine-tenths of wealth produced) or in Iraq (where chaos still reigns), unless accompanied by an effective civil society—which can only come from the society itself.

Those who reject such an evolution toward democracy will remain aggressive and will be treated as such by the market democracies.

Deterring Aggressive Regimes

Faced with permanently aggressive states, dissuasion will always be necessary and its absence always disastrous. In October 1936, confronted by the remilitarization of the Ruhr by Nazi troops, Lord Halifax and Léon Blum failed to react—and war followed. In October 1962, following the installation of Soviet missiles in Cuba and their rejection by the Kennedy brothers, peace remained unbroken. At the beginning of the eighties, then French president François Mitterrand supported the installation of American rockets in Europe, thus helping to dispel the Soviet threat.

Similarly, both today and tomorrow, those who wish to live free in market democracies will be unable to accept the presence, directly confronting them, of offensive weapons controlled by groups openly calling for their destruction.

No one will be safe from weapons at first aimed at other targets. Now pointed at Japan, North Korea's missiles will one day target the United States and China. The missiles of a Pakistan fallen into the hands of fundamentalists will threaten first India, then Europe. Those of Hezbollah — in other words Iran — that now target Israel will one day be pointed (from Beirut or Tehran) at Cairo, Riyadh, Algiers, Tunis, Casablanca, Istanbul, then at Rome, Madrid, London, and Paris. Should the battle lines harden and the country be threatened with annihilation, China's missiles could one day target Japan and the United States.

Democracies must not let themselves be impressed by such threats. If, out of fear of reprisals, they accept the permanent targeting of their countries by Iranian, Pakistani, or Korean missiles, they will be entering a fool's game, like that played by France and Great Britain in 1936, then in 1938 at Munich. And the stakes will be even higher, for these weapons could be launched from fifteen different sites by fifteen different dictatorial regimes and at different targets. To eliminate them, the Alliance must first threaten the regimes concerned with preventive action, make clear its own strike capabilities, and intimidate its enemies into backing down. If this is not enough to make the threats disappear, it must strike.

Preventive Action

No dissuasion will be possible against pirates, because they will have no territory to defend. Yielding to them in one place will not suffice to calm them. Mafias would not be satisfied with control of Colombia or Afghanistan; Islamic extremists would not stop at the destruction of Israel, nor with American withdrawal from Iraq or Saudi Arabia.

Against pirates, only preventive attack will suffice. The Alliance and every one of its members must therefore prepare to launch preventive war on those of the pirates (or on those of the nations where they have sought refuge) who threaten to use their weapons in the service of a faith, of a secular ambition, or in the search for criminal profit. To justify such a preventive war, the Alliance must not dream up bellicose intentions on the part of its adversary, nor take as an excuse imaginary weapons of mass destruction, as was the case with the war against Iraq in 2003. The Alliance cannot found its foreign policy on human rights yet violate them daily. But at some point in this century it may have to do so.

Optimists will say that this saber-rattling should not be taken too seriously. A country, or a nonstate entity, that achieves nuclear-power status or possesses extremely murderous weapons will of necessity turn reasonable. The best proof of this is that all those that have disclosed (officially or unofficially) their possession of such arsenals have so far indeed turned "reasonable."

The optimists are partly right. Democracies, where power is controlled by public opinion, or totalitarian regimes that have suffered painfully from war, will never make offensive use of these weapons. But the higher the number of players in the strategic game, the higher the number of those urged on by madmen or by those for whom death (of others, including their own troops) will not count. Then the chances of seeing these arms used will rise.

So the world will live increasingly haunted by fear of nuclear annihilation, of miniaturized war, of suicidal war. It is true that four kinds of conflict will erupt before hyperconflict: wars triggered by scarcity, frontier wars, wars for influence, wars between pirates and sedentaries.

Wars of Scarcity: Petroleum and Water

Just as wars have been fought over coal and iron, so they will be fought for petroleum and rare materials. First (and as it has been for a century), the need for a steady petroleum supply will provoke a number of conflicts as its extraction becomes costlier and more difficult. The United States, which consumes a quarter of the world's oil (with nearly two-thirds of it coming from abroad), will be determined to retain control of its sources of supply. It will want to go on controlling Saudi Arabia and Iraq; it will also want to recover control of Iran to prevent a blocking of the Strait of Ormuz, which would deprive the planet of a fifth of world production and drive the cost of a barrel of oil skyward. The American presence in the Central Asian nations of Kazakhstan and Uzbekistan will be substantially reinforced, at once to monitor what is happening in Iran and to prevent China from laying hands on the region. The United States will exercise more and more control over the Gulf of Mexico and ensure that Canada, Mexico, and Venezuela at least have compliant leaders. Conflicts could also flare, based on the petroleum pretext, in Central Asia between China and Russia, between the United States and China, between Turkey and Iran. Kazakhstan will step forward as an arbiter and as a regional power. The other major consumer countries (the European Union, Japan, China, and India) will also want to retain access to the oilfields of the Middle East, Russia, Africa, and Central Asia, as well as control of the zones through which this oil reaches the sea.

On Russia's borders (a zone crisscrossed by pipelines), pitiless civil wars (often financed by rival oil companies) will ravage these transit regions.

For the same reasons, Venezuela, Nigeria, Congo, and Indonesia, whose oilfields will one day be exhausted without their even having time to build modern economies around them, could also become (or become again) conflict zones.

Finally, the maritime areas (where future major fields will be found and where fleets of tankers will transit) will be so many sites of possible clashes.

Drinking water—rarer and rarer, as we have seen—will also provoke increasingly significant wars. In the last fifty years, thirty-seven conflicts have been waged over it, always on a local scale. This can only repeat itself: 145 nations have a part of their territory situated over a transborder water basin; around a third of the 263 transborder basins are shared by more than two countries; nineteen basins involve at least five countries. Brazil, Argentina, Paraguay, and Uruguay are competing for the world's third-largest underground freshwater reserve, the Guarani basin. The Danube basin is shared by eighteen nations: the periodic Balkan crises are partly rooted in this region. Tomorrow, when drinking water starts to run short, these battles will become much more violent. India, short of water, might contemplate diverting the three biggest rivers born there, which now enter the sea in Bangladesh. If Lebanon installs pumps on the El Ouazzane watercourse, a tributary of the Jordan feeding the Sea of Galilee and currently supplying Israel with a third of its drinking water, conflict will surely ensue. Turkey's plans to control the waters of the Euphrates and Tigris rivers will worry Syria and Iraq. Tajikistan, Kyrgyzstan, Kazakhstan, Uzbekistan, and Turkmenistan will quarrel increasingly over the Amu Darya and Sir Darya rivers, essential to the intensive cultivation of cotton. Hydroelectric dams in China—where the Mekong River is born—will threaten Vietnam, Cambodia, and Thailand. Mexico and the United States will quarrel over the Colorado and Rio Grande. Senegal and Mauritania may fight one another over control of the Senegal River. Algeria, Libya, and Chad might also come to blows over exploitation of their rare transborder water layers. Albania, Greece, and Macedonia risk entering into conflict for the same reasons. Finally—and above all—ten states share the waters of the Nile: Ethiopia, upstream, which supplies 86 percent of the flow and uses only 0.3 percent of it, intends to build thirty-six dams. This would partly desiccate Egypt, in all likelihood provoking an immediate conflict.

Finally, climatic disturbances will ignite wars over occupation of lands that have remained or become breathable and cultivatable. Siberia, Morocco, Algeria, and southern Spain could become battlefields between natives and immigrants.

Border Wars: From the Middle East to Africa

Several countries could well fight their neighbors in order to reunite populations, such as India and Pakistan over control of Kashmir, and between very many countries of sub-Saharan Africa in order to bring ethnic groups together.

Others will also try to destroy a neighbor. Several Arab countries still want to liquidate the Jewish state — which must therefore win every war against them on pain of annihilation. Diehards in the region will in any case unleash hostilities as soon as a peace agreement between Israel and its neighbors is announced.

The victory of democracy will also give birth to new conflicts within nations — either to challenge domination by one ethnic group, to provoke secession, or to avoid it. Today, more than forty conflicts of this kind are going on in twenty-seven countries. Some of them have dragged on for decades, most of them in Africa and Asia. The struggles ravaging Côte d'Ivoire, Darfur, Kashmir, Congo, and Sri Lanka are the most murderous of them. Congo long since surpassed a death toll of three million.

If these nations cannot organize their acts of partition in a spirit of calm, as the Soviet Union and Czechoslovakia did in 1992, the world will be headed toward civil wars that will end with the creation of new states, as in India and Yugoslavia, or in widespread ruin, as in Rwanda, Transnistria, Somaliland, Côte d'Ivoire, or Ethiopia. Conflicts of this kind could erupt in Congo, Russia, and Central Asia (between Russia, Georgia, Armenia, Turkey, and Iran), in Senegal, India, China, Indonesia. and the Philippines. Probably the worst of these clashes will be that opposing Ibos and Hausas in Nigeria.

Other conflicts of this same kind could take place between various groups within the bosom of developed countries. Even cities will proclaim secession; ethnic or linguistic minorities will demand independence. The partitioning of territories will go badly.

We must therefore expect many civil wars and thus, as always, the designation of scapegoats for elimination. As always, genocides will then be committed with the crudest of weapons. At least three of these massacres—against the Armenians, Jews, and Tutsi—were perpetrated in the twentieth century. Many others will take place in the twenty-first. And those who do not believe it have only to remember that in 1938 no one thought the Shoah would be possible.

Wars of Influence

As in the past, some countries will go so far as to make war on their neighbors to maintain their rank, distract domestic opinion from internal concerns, or else to wage an ideological or religious war.

Iran or Pakistan, for example, could commit themselves to war in order to take control of the region extending from Palestine to the Chinese frontier. Nigeria could attempt to take control of raw materials in neighboring countries by occupying them; Kazakhstan could fight Turkey for control of the Turkish-speaking countries in the region. As has often been the case in the past, Russia might make war to avoid encirclement — this time by Asian allies of the United States as well as by China and Islam. China could fight to recapture Taiwan, to control Kazakhstan, to occupy Siberia, or to allow a single party under stress to hold on to power. The United States might go to war to defend Taiwan, Israel, or Europe against weapons aimed at them from Iran, Egypt, or the Maghreb. India might fight to control its border regions and destroy the rear bases of Muslim rebels. Australia could go to war to thwart its neighbors' ambitions, such as Indonesia and China.

Wars Between Pirates and Sedentaries

Pirates have attacked the sedentary since the dawn of humanity. They have done so in the name of money, faith, poverty, a national ideology, or ambition, and they show absolutely no respect for human life. The Roman Empire died at their hands, and the mercantile order too seems likely to succumb.

As in remotest antiquity, on all the seas, piracy (whether criminal or political) will continue to disrupt relations between sedentary groups. According to the rare statistics available, incidents of maritime piracy increased fivefold between 1995 and 2006. That figure will continue to rise, especially around the Malacca Strait, which channels almost half of the world's petroleum, and on the Caribbean, where more and more drug-laden ships are on the move. The Mediterranean will also return to being a major zone for piratical exactions—which will also occur along the axes crossing the deserts and in densely populated neighborhoods of big cities in both South and North.

Piracy will go on attacking the mass-tourism sites of virtual nomads. Everything that moves will be considered at once a target and a weapon—airplane, truck, train, ship, and every kind of communications network.

The pirates—religious, nihilist, or simply criminal—will strike the sedentary by surprise with the aim of instilling fear. They will not only seek to grab booty, but also to cut pipelines, close straits, stop all trade, all commerce, tourism, and traffic. They will attack the lands—real and virtual—of the empire with viruses—real and virtual—transforming their first victims into nomadic weapons sowing death around them. They will seek to disarticulate surveillance systems and so terrify the sedentary that they stop moving about altogether, ceasing to plan ahead, to create, to entertain themselves. The sedentary will shut themselves off in their bunkers.

The pirates will use all the weapons of modern corporations, with vanguards, local groups, "circuses," and "theaters."

Some of these pirates (and not only among religiously inspired movements) will have recourse to suicide attacks. The first attacks of this kind were by

Russian nihilists of the late nineteenth century, and then by Japanese forces during the Second World War, followed more recently by Tamil freedom fighters in Sri Lanka. Mafias have already used the suicide weapon, setting off unwilling human bombs. Islamist terrorists have used them in Europe and the Middle East, particularly in Iraq, Lebanon, and Israel. The attacks in Kenya in 2000, in New York on September 11, 2001, then in Casablanca, Madrid, and London are an integral part of this story, without constituting either a break with the past or a change of nature.

One day (perhaps not as distant as we think) poverty-driven pirates without theological motives will blow themselves up in European city centers. We shall witness convoys of suicide ships from the southern hemisphere blown up in the open Mediterranean and Caribbean, live before the television cameras.

The masters of the polycentric world, then of super-empire, will strive to fight such acts by transforming the defensive military Alliance into a world police organization. Mercenaries, paid by the Alliance, will destroy the pirates' fallback bases, fight house to house in neighborhoods occupied by mafia gangs, and intercept their raids before they reach their objectives. They will trick them into killing one another and draw down on them the anger of the infranomads. The civilian population will be caught between the two lines of fire.

As noted, at this tempo, it will not be tomorrow's Africa that will one day resemble today's West, but the whole West that could tomorrow evoke today's Africa.

Hyperconflict

When the polycentric world begins to unravel, when corsairs, pirates, private armies, mercenaries, and terrorists attempt to take over, totalitarian regimes will slaughter one another to establish supremacy without acknowledging any law of war or even any arbitrator. Countries of the North will form alliances with those of the South, while Islamist terrorists will join forces with drug cartels. There will simultaneously be hot wars and cold wars, private wars and state wars. Police and armed forces will mingle with one another without respecting the most elementary rules of warfare. Civilian populations will be helpless prey, as was the case in World War II. The religions of the Book will fight one another, to the greater glory of their enemies. Some theologians will see in this the advent of the battle signaling, in the Book, the end of days — an end (for the Jews) that must lead to the arrival of the Messiah. For Christians, it is linked with His return; for certain Muslims, with the hidden Imam; for Hindus, it is marked by the advent of Kalki, Vishnu's tenth and final incarnation. In all cases, they say, it will end with the victory of good over evil.

If (once super-empire is in place) all these sources of conflict come together one day in a single battle, if all the players we have so far mentioned see their interests served by going one after another into the same confrontation, hyperconflict could then be unleashed. It might be triggered in Taiwan, Mexico, or the Middle East. All three are points of confluence of the major conflicts over water, oil, religions, demography, the North-South gap and frontier disputes. It could also be triggered by a lightning attack on the West by an Iran in alliance with Pakistan, which will both have become Islamic nuclear powers.

No institution would then be capable of negotiating compromises or jamming the machinery. The world would become an immense battlefield where nations, mercenary peoples, terrorists, pirates, democracies, dictatorships, tribes, nomadic mafias, and the religious would crash into one another, some fighting for money, others for the faith, land, or freedom.

Every weapon we have earlier discussed could then be used. Humanity, which since the sixties has possessed the ability to commit collective suicide, might well use them, in which case there will be no one left to write history, which is never anything but the thinking of the strongest. This is of course a worst-case scenario, but nothing is impossible here: man's tragedy is that when he can do something, in the end he will always do it.

And yet, well before humanity has thus put an end to its history—at least I would like to believe this—the failure of super-empire and the threat of hyperconflict will compel the democracies to find sufficient motivation to vanquish the pirates, the nonstate entities, and the rogue states, and suppress their own death wish.

The more optimistic—and more likely—view is that Alliance's armies will sweep the dictators aside; the drug cartels will be tamed, big corporations will no longer gamble their future on the growth of military orders; all religions will calm down and become forces for peace, reason, and tolerance. Already at work, new forces will seize power in order to create a just, pacific, united, and brotherly world.

And then, as happened after the fall of the Roman Empire, there will be a rebirth—on the ruins of a promising past spoiled by an excessively long series of mistakes—a mighty longing to live, joyful interbreedings, jubilant transgressions. From them new civilizations will surge forth, made of the residue of nations bled dry and of super-empire in escheat, nourished on new values.

A planetary democracy will be enthroned, limiting the market's powers. It will try to win other, much more urgent, wars: against the madness of men, against climatic upheaval, against mortal disease, alienation, and poverty.

Now the third wave of the future will roll in, that of *hyperdemocracy*. Here is a brief sketch of its history.

6

Third Wave of the Future: Planetary Democracy

At the end of his last book, *Critique of the Gotha Program* (a commentary on the draft program of the United Workers' Party of Germany), Karl Marx wrote this mysterious phrase in Latin: *"Dixi et salvavi animam meam"* (I say that only to save my soul). As though he wanted his readers to understand that in his view the program he had just proposed to the German socialists had not the slightest chance of being implemented, as though he thought that no one, ever, would have the courage or the means of mastering capitalism and its consequences, at once inspiring and suicidal.

Today, at a time when market democracies have traveled a large part of the road predicted by the author of *Das Kapital*, and when socialism has gone astray in many of the dead ends foreseen and denounced by Marx, the long-term survival of a free, happy, diverse, equitable humankind, concerned for dignity and respect, seems impossible. It even seems vain to think about it.

And yet when Thomas More dreamed in 1516 of having the leaders of Utopia, his imaginary city, elected to office, he had no idea that four centuries later the ministers of his own country would be chosen by the whole people. And when in July 1914 Jean Jaurès dreamed of a free, democratic, peaceful, and united Europe, there was nothing to suggest that such would be the Old Continent's situation less than eighty years later.

Today we must perform the same act of faith in the future. Try once again to show that humanity is not doomed to destroy itself—neither through the market, nor science, nor by war, and above all not by stupidity or malevolence.

Everything seems to promise a progressive transformation of man into object, an amplification of injustices, insecurity, violence. Everything even indicates that we are entering a dark eve-of-war phase. The most sophisticated nations react to barbarism with barbarism, to fear with selfishness, to terror with reprisals. It even seems reasonable to resign ourselves to admitting that man is a mere monster, and that our world will never become a planetary democracy, tolerant, peaceable, diverse but united. Yet such a dynamic is already on the march: goodness, after the market and war—Jupiter after Quirinus and Mars.

To save humankind from its demons, this third wave of the future must obviously break before one or other of the two preceding waves makes an end, each in its own way, of the human species.

To conceive how such a future could arrive in time, we must—like the visionaries of the past—look very far ahead, far beyond the present supremacy of the American empire, the threatening emergence of the polycentric order, beyond super-empire and the countless conflicts that will follow. Then we will understand how what I call hyperdemocracy fits naturally into this history of the future. We will see that many forces are working underground to lay its foundations, and that it depends only on us for it to become — in a few decades — the world's reality.

Democratic Shock

As with the dawn of every major revolution, we must first determine how urgently matters stand and who the players are. We must also define the revolution's values and picture what its institutions may be, in the modesty of daily life and the immoderate passion of the ideal.

Countless positive forces are today working toward the achievement of a world everyone can live in — the dizzying discoveries of the sciences and our amazing technical advances will foster a growing awareness in a growing number of people that the world is a village, that abundance is conceivable, that it is possible for everyone to live longer and much better.

We could rationally deduce from all this that the climate can be stabilized, that water and energy can be found in abundance, that obesity and stark poverty can disappear, that nonviolence is attainable, that prosperity for everyone is a realistic goal, that democracy can become universal, that businesses can serve the common good, that we can even envisage protecting all the differences and creating other ones.

Yet awareness of these possibilities would not be enough to forestall the advent of super-empire nor avoid hyperconflict. Man has never built anything on a foundation of good tidings.

On the other hand, a few of the catastrophes already foreseen will demonstrate crudely to the most skeptical that our present way of life cannot last. Climatic upheavals, increasing obesity and the use of drugs, the stranglehold of violence on daily life, more and more terrifying acts by terrorists, the impossible gated seclusion of the wealthy, the mediocrity of our entertainments, the dictatorship of insurance companies, the invasion of time by market goods, the scarcity of water and oil, the rise of urban delinquency, the increasing frequency of financial crises, waves of immigrants washed ashore on our beaches (first with outstretched hands, then with raised fists), increasingly murderous and selective technologies, the moral bankruptcy of the wealthiest will one day come along to wake the deepest sleepers. Once more, disasters will be the most eloquent advocates for change.

As at the end of any great war, people will then speak once again of drawing lessons from the past, of forgiving without forgetting, of building a different world, of doing away with violence forever. People of every social condition, of all cultures and religious affiliations, will ponder the possibilities for humanity's long-term survival. They will realize that neither super-empire nor hyperconflict can create a world built to last. Political plans will spring forth from everywhere for settling border disputes, reconciling manifold national claims within the same territory, and teaching people how to live serenely with themselves and others.

These utopian plans will perhaps be briefly taken over by dictators dreaming of founding a peaceful and planetary empire. A new totalitarian ideology, all-encompassing, reassuring, messianic, religious or secular, will doubtless have its prophet, its book, its priests, its police, its butchers. Then a new, harmonious organization of the world will see the light of day. At first, it will merely be a planetary cohabitation of market and democracy. A little later, both will be overtaken by what I shall call hyperdemocracy.

To help understand this prognosis, I must here introduce some new concepts.

Vanguard players (I shall call them *transhumans*) will run (they are already running) *relational enterprises* in which profit will be no more than a hindrance, not a final goal. Each of these transhumans will be altruistic, a citizen of the planet, at once nomadic and sedentary, his neighbor's equal in rights and obligations, hospitable and respectful of the world. Together, transhumans will give birth to planetary institutions and change the course of industrial enterprises. For the benefit of each individual, they will develop *essential goods* (the most important being a *good time*), and for the general benefit a *common good* (whose chief dimension will be a *collective intelligence*).

Then, even beyond a new global balance between market and democracy, between public services and corporations, transhumans will give birth to a new order of abundance, from which the market will be gradually excluded in favor of the relational economy.

All this may seem utterly improbable. None of the agents of these changes seems even to exist. Here again, this is not for the first time. When Marx spoke in 1848 of the imminent victory of the bourgeoisie and the coming power of the working class, Europe possessed practically no bourgeoisie and no working class. Even before they emerged, he had identified history's future players. This is again our task today.

The Vanguard of Hyperdemocracy: Transhumans and Relational Enterprises

When a convoy is on the move, its vanguard includes many more people than the generals lolling in the midst of their troops. History bifurcates only when adventurous beings, concerned with their freedom and the defense of their values, advance the cause of men (generally to their own great regret). In the mercantile order, this vanguard has until now been composed, core by core (as we have seen), of what I have called the "innovative class"—entrepreneurs, inventors, artists, financiers, political leaders.

In the future, a part of this class—individuals particularly sensitive to this question of the future—will realize that their happiness depends on that of others, that the human species can only survive united and pacific. They will cease to belong to the mercantile innovative class, and refuse to put themselves at the service of pirates. They will become what I call transhumans.

Altruistic, conscious of the history of the future, concerned by the fate of their contemporaries and their descendants, anxious to help, to understand, to leave behind them a better world, transhumans will reject the selfishness of the hypernomads and the destructive fury of the pirates. They will not believe that they own the world, merely recognizing that they only hold it in trust.

They will be ready to put into practice the virtues of the sedentary (vigilance, hospitality, a sense of the long term) and those of the nomad (obstinacy, memory, intuition). They will feel at once citizens of the world and members of several communities. Their nationalities will be those of the languages they speak, and no longer simply of the countries where they will live. For them, rebellion against the unavoidable will be the rule, the insolence of optimism will be their moral standard, and brotherhood will suffice for ambition. They will find their happiness in the pleasure of giving pleasure, particularly to children they know they are responsible for. They will learn again that transmission is peculiar to man.

Women will become transhumans more easily than men: finding pleasure in giving pleasure is peculiar to motherhood. The progressive rise of women in every dimension of the economy and of society—particularly through microfinance—will add enormously to the number of transhumans. Among today's transhumans, we might cite both Melinda Gates and Mother Teresa. We will also find among them billionaires who have entrusted the bulk of their fortunes to a foundation, as well as social innovators, teachers, creators, religious and secular women, and quite simply people of good will. People for whom the Other is a value in himself.

While in the world of scarcity, in other words in the market, the Other is a rival (the enemy come to quarrel over scarce goods, the one against whom freedom is built and with whom no knowledge must be shared), for transhumans the Other will be first and foremost the witness of his own existence, the way of verifying that he is not alone. The Other will allow him to talk, transmit, prove generous, loving, outstripping himself, creating more than will satisfy his own needs and more than he believes himself capable of creating. The Other will allow him to understand that love of the Other, and therefore first of himself, is the condition of humanity's survival.

Cheek by jowl with the market economy, in which everyone measures himself against the Other, transhumans will usher in an economy of altruism, of free availability, of mutual giving, of public service, of the general interest. This economy, which I call "relational," will not obey the laws of scarcity: transmitting knowledge does not deprive its transmitter. This economy will make it possible to produce and exchange truly free services—recreation, health, education, human relations, and so forth—that each one will deem it good to offer the Other and to produce with no further remuneration than respect, gratitude, jubilation. These services are not scarce, for the more one gives, the more one receives. The more one gives, the more one has the desire and the means to give. Working, even in the relational economy, will become a boundless pleasure.

We may also hope for the reinforcement of states, the socialization of public spending, the enhanced capacities of armies to fight against piracy, better systems for rights to property. And, for the poorest, products manufactured by the market, from clothing to housing, from food to the telephone, from credit to insurance, will be widely available.

Transhumans will constitute a new innovative class, bearers of social and artistic innovations rather than solely mercantile offerings.

Transhumans will perfect the instruments of their

project. Just as the market's driving spirits create industrial firms that allocate scarce resources, transhumans will favor relational enterprises that allocate essentially unlimited resources. Their final objective will be to improve the world's lot, treating problems the market cannot solve, counterbalancing the globalization of the market with the globalization of democracy. In such firms, profit will be only a constraint necessary for survival, not a final goal.

Political parties and unions are the first relational businesses. The Red Cross, Doctors Without Borders, CARE, Greenpeace, the World Wildlife Fund (WWF), and above all many other nongovernmental organizations (NGOs) created in Asia, Latin America, or Africa, such as Grameen, have taken up the challenge. To mention just one of the latter (from among the thousands that exist), I would cite the NGO that made it possible for a shantytown in Lima—Villa El Salvador—to enroll 90 percent of its children and grownups in school. Situated on the margins of capitalism, these relational enterprises are already playing the part the merchants of Bruges and Venice played on the margins of feudalism. Soon we shall find all kinds of institutions fulfilling civic, medical, ecological, or social missions (NGOs, intermediaries in diplomatic negotiations, amateur sports clubs, free-of-charge or cooperative meeting places or sites). Most will be created in the South by people who will act without expecting anything more from anyone. One of the most important categories in relational enterprises will be made up of microfinance institutions, increasingly major players in the market, democracy, and human relations.

The production of relational enterprises—evaluated in mercantile terms—already represents 10 percent of world GDP, and that share is increasing very rapidly. They have already created concepts seen as harbingers of the future's values—the right to intervene, the right to a childhood, the right to dignity. They are also at the origins of the most recent international institutions: the AIDS Fund, the International Criminal Court, the World Environment Program. Thanks to these very special institutions, we are starting to speak of an *international community* (although not yet of a *world government*) and of the protection of nature (although not yet of a *common good*). Here already are the first babblings of a world democracy, which I call hyper-democracy. New relational firms will appear, above all in urban management, education, health, the fight against poverty, environmental management, the protection of women, equitable trade, balanced nutrition, the valorization of what is free, social reinsertion, the war on drugs, and monitoring of the monitors. They will take the place of private enterprises and public services: they will take charge of disease prevention, the social reinsertion of the marginalized, arranging access for the weakest to essential goods (particularly education), and conflict resolution. New professions will emerge from within these firms. A new attitude to work will develop, consisting of finding pleasure in giving—making people smile, transmitting, relieving, and consoling.

Together, these relational enterprises will make up a new economy, as marginal today as capitalism at the start of the thirteenth century, and just as clearly a harbinger of the future.

The Institutions of Hyperdemocracy

Before the middle of the twenty-first century, hyperdemocracy will begin to make itself known in the institutional reality of the world. We shall begin to debate the installation of coherent global institutions, making it possible for humanity to avoid succumbing to the assaults of super-empire and to avoid the potential ravages of hyperconflict.

It would serve no purpose to attempt to describe these institutions in detail. Too much time will have gone by before their day dawns, too many storms will break, too many technologies will emerge. And too many surprises will come along to divert (temporarily) the course of history.

But we can sketch its broad outlines without too much danger of making a mistake, from a knowledge of past history and of the first two waves of the future.

These future institutions will be made up of a grab bag of local, national, continental, and global organizations. Within their bosom, each human being will be worth as much and be as influential as any other.

The city will be the principal living space of the bulk of humanity. Hundreds of cities will be more heavily populated in 2100 than a hundred countries today. Since more than two-thirds of humanity will live there, gigantic sums will be required for their infrastructure. The city will be the area of the biggest collective investments and the principal tax collector. Urban planning will become a major science. Digital infrastructure will help make the city a site for encounters, for trading, for living. Using the technologies of nomadic ubiquity, a participative and associative democracy will connect all who live there, all who work there, all who will be its users or who will in one way or another be affected by its development. Whole neighborhoods will arise there autonomically.

To fight off the assaults of the market, states will need to focus on a few sovereign functions: security, public order, freedom, defense of language, universal access for both permanent and transient residents to health and knowledge, the right to a training-indexed minimum income. To fulfill these functions equitably, states (like cities) will be subsidized if necessary on a continental and even global scale. Borders will fade away. Everyone will be a citizen of several entities at once, and it will become possible to defend one's identity without seeking to destroy one's neighbor's. Nations will little by little succeed in finding the conditions favorable to pacific coexistence. New forms of democratic control will appear, based on autonomous regulatory agencies, permanently monitoring the work of elected officials thanks to the methods of nomadic ubiquity and of hypersurveillance.

Each continent or subcontinent will group its market democracies in a union, as the European Union has already done. Each such union will be responsible for its currency, the transparency of its markets, the harmonization of its members' social conditions, environmental protection, domestic security, civil rights, health, education, immigration, foreign policy, and regional defense. It must create for itself a continental parliament and government. It must also possess (as is already the case with Europe) a body empowered to resolve conflicts between nations of the same continent. Such a future could become possible, especially in the Middle East, which must one day unite all its nations—including Israel and Palestine—in a regional union. The European Union, standard-bearer of hyperdemocracy, will become a nation of a new kind, probably expanding one day to include Turkey and Russia. It is there that the conditions for equilibrium between market and democracy will best be met. It is in Europe that hyperdemocracy will begin.

New institutions must be created—will be created—on a global scale, expanding those already in existence. The United Nations will be their base. A Constitution for the planet will pick up and extend the current United Nations Charter. For this to happen, the UN will have to assume a supranational (and no longer just multilateral) dimension. Its preamble will list all the rights and duties of every human in relation to nature, to other humans, and to life. It will include rights not foreseen in the present charter, especially the new right—essential, groundbreaking—to a decent childhood, with implications for the duties of parents. Other rights and obligations will mandate the protection of life, nature, and diversity, and will impose absolute boundaries on the market.

The UN General Assembly, which will include more and more states, will be progressively supported first by a second chamber, where leaders elected by universal suffrage will each represent an equal number of human beings, and then by a third chamber, where mercantile and relational enterprises will foregather. This global parliament will collect taxes, based on each member country's GDP, its weapons budget, and its greenhouse gas emissions.

The UN Security Council will merge with the G8 and will expand to include a few of the Eleven, including India, Brazil, and Indonesia. It will later be made up solely of representatives of the continental unions.

The Security Council will serve as the executive body of a planetary government built around the current secretary-general. This planetary government will devote many more resources to the protection of humanity than all the planet's governments do today. It will dictate social norms—such as the principle of the best possible world social regime—which it will gradually impose on all the world's business enterprises. It will give itself the means to make them respect it.

International financial institutions, such as the World Trade Organization (WTO) and the International Labor Organization (ILO) will be brought directly under its trusteeship, so that they will no longer obey exclusively the instructions of the wealthiest countries. This planetary government will acquire the military means for fighting mafias, the drug trade, sexual exploitation, slavery, climate upheaval, disposal of waste, and attacks (accidental, terrorist, or military) by nanorobots and other self-replicating pathogens that could destroy the biomass—a *blue jelly* (the ultimate nanotechnological weapon) held exclusively by the planetary government, will be used in order to combat the gray jelly. A planetary assistance and security force with the best equipment (discussed above) will protect the environment and combat piracy.

To support this world government, new organs for control, defense, and regulation will step by step take up a position stemming from the governance bodies of super-empire and those of relational enterprises: a planetary criminal court will ensure the compatibility of laws enacted on each continent and try the most dangerous pirates; a global authority will ensure the availability of water; a global department of labor will prevent monopolies and require compliance with worker rights. Another authority will verify the quality of consumer goods, in particular of food. Still another will oversee the major insurance companies, other governance bodies, and the very big businesses essential to life. This latter authority will possess the means to combat the pirate economy and to defend intellectual and personal property.

A central bank will ensure the stability of the principal currencies, then will manage a single currency. It will exclude from the international financial community any institution permitting drug-money laundering. A global development bank will finance major infrastructure projects in cities and countries that respect the planetary Constitution. It will support countries that convert their drug- or organized-crime-dependent economies and will reinforce them in their war against pirates. A specialist institution will help structure relational businesses and verify that they are not covers for pirate or terrorist organizations. Another planetary institution will focus on the development of microfinance.

Obviously, the headquarters of these institutions will not all have to be located in the same place — even though we spoke earlier of Jerusalem for some of them, as the capital of believers in the god shared by half mankind, the god of Abraham. Their lives may be as nomadic as the super-empire it will be their mission to counterbalance.

The Market's Place in Hyperdemocracy

Market and democracy will thus gradually restore a planetary equilibrium. On the one hand, hyperdemocracy's institutions will allow the market to function effectively and to avoid the underemployment of productive capacities by launching major worldwide energy, digital, and urban infrastructure projects. On the other hand, the market — regulated and globalized — will stop penetrating the sanctuary of democracy. It will even find it in its own interest to develop tools to serve democracy and to create urban infrastructure, antipollution methodologies, and methods for fighting obesity and poverty. New technologies will make possible a new abundance of energy and water within a protected environment and stabilized climate. Architects and urban planners will invent cities on a human scale; artists will raise awareness that the world's beauty deserves protection and development.

Microcredit will dominate the banking system. Mercantile relational businesses (that is to say, businesses having profit as a final goal and human relations as a by-product) will provide personal services (from health to education by way of entertainment) and at-home services (including assistance to populations in difficulty, the elderly and infirm). Markets will redirect technical progress toward the health industries, in particular the food industry, as well as toward knowledge and the environment. They will value lived time rather than stored time, and services rather than industrial products. They will offer the presentation of stored time free of charge, and will require payment for live entertainment. Movies will be presented gratis, and film buffs will pay to see the same actors onstage. Music files will be free, and music lovers will pay to attend concerts. Books and periodicals will be free, and readers will pay the publishers for the privilege of debating their authors and hearing them speak. Publishers will sell lectures given by their authors and books of very high quality. Such costlessness will come to permeate all fields essential to life.

The relational economy and the market will each have much to gain from the other's success. The relational economy will have everything to gain from the most effective possible functioning of the market, while the market's effectiveness will depend crucially on the social climate engendered by the relational economy. And finally, the market's major business entities will increasingly be judged, by their own shareholders, according to their capacity to serve the general interest and to promote relational activities.

The Collective Result of Hyperdemocracy: The Common Good and Universal Intelligence

Hyperdemocracy will develop a *common good*, which will create *collective intelligence*.

Humanity's common good, the ultimate objective of hyperdemocracy, will be neither greatness, nor wealth, nor even happiness, but protection of the things that make life possible and worthwhile—climate, air, water, freedom, democracy, culture, languages, fields of knowledge . . . This common good will be like a library that needs to be updated and maintained, a natural park, to be passed on after cultivating and enriching it without having modified it in any irreversible way. The way in which Namibia fosters its wildlife, or France protects its forests, or in which certain peoples protect their culture, suggests what might be a foretaste of this common good. This can never be a market commodity, nor a state property, nor a multilateral good: it must be a *supranational good.*

The chief intellectual dimension of the common good will be a *universal intelligence* peculiar to the human species, and different from the sum of human intelligences.

The collective intelligence of a group is not the sum of the knowledge of its members, nor even the sum of their capacities to think: it is an intelligence peculiar to itself, which thinks differently from each member of the group. Thus a network of neurons becomes a learning machine; a telephone grid performs other functions than those of each telephone exchange; a computer thinks differently from each microprocessor. A city is a being distinct from each of its inhabitants; an orchestra is something beyond the sum of its musicians; a play is different from the role played by each actor; and the results of research are worth more than the contribution of each researcher working on the project. All collective intelligence is the result of bridges, of links between individual intelligences, essential for creating the new.

In the same way, humanity creates a collective intelligence, universal, distinct from the sum of the particular intelligences of the beings who make it up, and distinct from the collective intelligences of groups or of nations.

The ultimate objective of this collective intelligence

will not be utilitarian. It will be unknowable, priceless. It will be able to translate itself in diverse works: numberless global cooperative networks will permit the creation of a corpus of knowledge and universal works of art, transcending the knowledge and the works of all who take part in them. In fact, this universal intelligence has existed forever in embryonic state. It has allowed the human species to survive through adaptation. With the arrival of new technologies, it is developing ever faster. It will create an entirely new relationship with intellectual property, which can be absolute no longer but must be shared with humanity as a whole, essential to each individual's creativity.

For example, the development of freeware will form an exemplar of universal intelligence as a kind of global brain network, a collective golem. Similarly, while Wikipedia at the moment is no more than a weak and often unreliable aggregate of the intelligences of its authors, we shall see in it (we are already seeing) the birth (made possible by the work of all) of a collective result different from what each contributor intended.

History will thus drive the integration of collective intelligences into a universal intelligence; it will also be endowed with a collective memory that will preserve and accumulate its knowledge. By its very nature, it will last at least as long as the human race.

Universal intelligence will even be able to conceive of machines in its own service, defending the common good on its behalf.

Universal intelligence may next bring about an intelligence peculiar to the species, a *hyperintelligence* that will act in its own interests, distinct from the interests of the universal intelligence of a single generation of human beings. Finally, at the ultimate stage of evolution, we might witness (we may already be witnessing) a *hyperintelligence of the living*, of which humanity will be but an infinitesimal component. This hyperintelligence of the living would no longer act solely in the interests of the human species.

And there the singular history of *Homo sapiens sapiens* would achieve consummation. Not in annihilation, as in the first two waves of the future, but simply in being overtaken.

The Individual Result of Hyperdemocracy: Essential Goods, Including *Good Times*

Hyperdemocracy will not attain only collective objectives. It will also allow each human being to achieve personal goals, unattainable through the market alone: to enjoy access to essential goods, in particular to *good times.*

Here I call *essential goods* all those to which each human being must have right of access in order to lead a worthwhile life, to participate in the common good. Among these essential goods are access to knowledge, housing, food, health care, work, water, air, security, freedom, equity, the networks, respect, the right to leave a place or to stay, compassion, solitude, living simultaneous passions, parallel truths, being surrounded by friends and family during one's last days.

This will lead to the suppression of any penalty that

involves the loss of civil rights, or is violent, or involves incarceration.

The chief essential good will thus be access to "good times." Times when everyone will watch not the spectacle of others' lives, but the reality of his or her own; in which everyone will be able to choose his model of success, to let his talents spread their wings, including those of whose existence we are as yet unaware. "Good times" will then mean living free, long, and young—and not in a hurry to "profit," as in the mercantile order.

These two goals—individual and collective—of hyperdemocracy will nourish one another: humankind's universal intelligence will increase with good times, which will be at everyone's disposal, and in return universal intelligence will create the conditions for everybody to enjoy "good times." Hyperdemocracy will function only among people enjoying access to essential goods.

Humankind's common good will be all the stronger as increasing numbers of people gain access to essential goods. Just as a research center has an interest in its researchers' discoveries, just as the speakers of one language need those who speak it to be as numerous as possible, so each human being will want others to be in full possession of the means to achieve their dignity and their freedom, in other words to be in good health and well educated. It will be in humanity's interest that each human be happy to be alive; altruism will be to everyone's benefit. Being transhuman will become rational.

The Hijacking of Hyperdemocracy

For long decades, super-empire will try to prevent the birth of hyperdemocracy. Some masters of the market, most of them hypernomads, will seek to undermine hyperdemocracy's values, hinder its attempts to create new institutions, and liquidate its players. They will denounce transhuman hypernomads as traitors. They will instill fear in them and attempt to corrupt them in an effort to make them change camps. Then, sensing the power of the wave, they will turn to specialist businesses in an effort to commercialize "relational nomadic objects" — companion robots, virtual fraternities, three-dimensional games simulating altruism, ersatz fair trade. They will sell what they too will call a "good time" — vacation time or time produced by nomadic objects that can be replicated on the assembly line. They will put "self-monitors" — supposedly designed to measure relational capacity — on the market. They will also invent relational prostheses and then clones — "artificial brothers" who make it possible for the user to have a stockpile of organs all to himself. The "happiness" of the clone will lie in helping the cloned one to survive.

Furthermore, some leaders of religious movements, theologians, gurus will attempt (are already attempting) to claim hyperdemocracy's concepts as their own. They will base their businesses on charity, mastery of time and meaning, costlessness, brotherhood, universal intelligence, "good times," the common good.

Some scientists will explain (they are already explaining) that inability to find a meaning in time, to prove oneself altruistic, is a disease curable by drugs or genetic manipulations of their own invention.

Finally, some politicians will try to put into place a more or less global dictatorship intended to create a "new man" fit to live in hyperdemocracy. They will argue that it will even be possible one day to conceive beings sufficiently masters of themselves to be immune to the urge to accumulate, to waste, to feel jealous—beings happy with others' happiness, programmed to love being what they are, freed even from all desire and all egoism.

I want to believe that one day—well before the end of the twenty-first century and in the wake of so many obstacles, dizzying precipices, and caricatures—super-empire will be sufficiently advanced to demonstrate the world's unity without destroying human identity. I also dare hope that hyperviolence will be so threatening to humanity that it will become aware of the need for a radical change of attitude toward itself. I am still convinced that transhumans will by then be sufficiently numerous and sufficiently organized to contain the first wave of the future and destroy the second.

I also dare to believe that dictatorships making a show of hyperdemocracy will endure for less time than those that once made a show of socialism. I want to believe, too, that religions will find a path to mutual tolerance and mutual enrichment.

And finally, I dare to believe that universal advances of the potential violence of the future I have sketched out earlier will contribute to making it impossible.

If such is the case, we shall see outlined the promise, beyond the vast upheavals to come, of an earth hospitable to all life's travelers.

Between now and then many events will have taken place, worse and better than those imagined here. Beauty will succeed in nourishing and protecting the last sparks of humanity. We will have written and shaped masterpieces, we will have discovered new concepts, we will have composed songs. Above all, we will have loved. And we will love again.

Index